TEXANS IN REVOLT
The Battle for San Antonio, 1835

TEXANS IN REVOLT

THE BATTLE FOR SAN ANTONIO, 1835

Alwyn Barr

UNIVERSITY OF TEXAS PRESS, AUSTIN

First Edition, 1990

Requests for permission to reproduce material from this work
should be sent to Permissions, University of Texas Press,
Box 7819, Austin, Texas 78713-7819.

∞ The paper used in this publication meets the minimum
requirements of American National Standard for Information
Sciences—Permanence of Paper for Printed Library Materials,
ANSI Z39.48–1984.

LIBRARY OF CONGRESS CATALOGING-IN-PUBLICATION DATA

Barr, Alwyn.
    Texans in revolt : the battle for San Antonio, 1835 / Alwyn
Barr. — 1st ed.
    p.   cm.
    Includes bibliographical references.
    ISBN 0-292-77042-1
    1. San Antonio (Tex.)—History—Siege, 1835.   I. Title.
F390.B339   1990
976.4'03—DC20   89-22585
                                                        CIP

CONTENTS

MAPS

PREFACE

Texans and other Americans have accepted with enthusiasm the San Jacinto battle cry: "Remember the Alamo! Remember Goliad!" Over fifty books have recounted aspects of the Alamo story, while at least fifteen others have focused upon Goliad or San Jacinto itself. At least fifteen films have offered versions of the three battles—most concerning the Alamo. The two moments of martyrdom and the history-shaping victory in 1836 have dominated the popular image of the Texas Revolution.

By contrast, the capture of San Antonio in 1835 has received far less attention. Yet the struggle for Béxar stands as the longest campaign of the Texas Revolution, the only major Texan success other than San Jacinto, and the victory at the end of 1835 that determined the pattern of military campaigns in 1836. To understand the Texas Revolution one must also remember San Antonio.

On a drive through the countryside between Gonzales and San Antonio, it is possible to envision the march of the Texans toward Béxar and their camps. Even near Concepción mission, where some open parkland remains along the San Antonio River, one can try to imagine the first major clash between the Mexican and Texan forces. Frustration grows when a modern historical marker for the Grass Fight cannot be located because of construction on the freeway that passes west of the downtown area. The effort becomes more difficult during a tour around the heart of San Antonio, where the plazas exist amid modern buildings, some towering overhead. In an automobile the distances seem short, and one is pressed to think in terms of men on foot or horseback. The Alamo, the Cos house in La Villita, and the Governor's Palace help recapture some sense of the original setting, despite their more recent surroundings. Yet a modern observer cannot envision the struggle for Béxar as easily as one might reconstruct some other military clashes by standing on the field of battle, as at San Jacinto or on the sites of some Civil War conflicts. Thus I have sought to develop a picture in words of the site and the soldiers and their struggle.

The first chapter of this study describes the two armies that fought at Béxar. Troops on both sides in the fall of 1835 differed to some extent from the soldiers who clashed the following spring. The Texans began as democratic volunteers from the Texas settlements, though the army came to include some United States volunteers—a group that claimed a greater role in the spring campaigns of 1836. Northern presidial troops formed a majority of the Mexican army, along with a smaller contingent of regulars—the soldiers who formed a majority when Santa Anna returned early the next year. Both armies brought combat experience with them. Some Mexican soldiers had fought in their revolution, in internal struggles, or on the frontier, while many Texans had served in earlier United States and Texan conflicts or against Indians. The roles of Stephen F. Austin and Martín Perfecto de Cos as commanders also receive attention. Neither army has been fully analyzed in earlier accounts of the campaign.

A second chapter follows the Texans' advance on Béxar in October. Before they arrived their leaders had halted to conduct a debate and to vote on whether to continue. Ambitions and revolutionary politics rivaled strategic views in the decision. Early skirmishes led to a Texas victory at Concepción, which provided both sides with a grasp of the greater firepower that Texan riflemen could generate under certain circumstances. The military politics and tactics of the Texan army have received only limited attention in previous discussions of the fighting at San Antonio. Sam Houston, James Bowie, and James W. Fannin appear in roles that offer insight into their later revolutionary careers.

The third chapter discusses cavalry clashes as well as renewed conflicts among the Texans over tactics in November. William Barret Travis and Thomas J. Rusk appear in important military roles in these weeks. Cold weather, boredom, ambitions, and the needs of the Texan cause took a toll on the early volunteers and their officers. Yet new men and leaders with fresh enthusiasm replaced them. Still the stubborn Mexican army held the town. The changing composition and mood of the Texan forces has not been fully developed before.

The last chapter recounts the final Texan debate about whether to advance or to retreat, which led to the attack on San Antonio in early December. The five days of fighting are described in detail to explore the shifting tides of hope and apprehension in both armies. Decisions by both commanders are analyzed. Two important aspects of the final struggle are revised from traditional accounts. The popular view has been that three hundred Texans captured Béxar from twelve hundred Mexicans. Instead, a reconstruction of the armies shows the Texans to have been slightly more numerous than the Mexicans until late in the fighting, when Cos received reinforcements who were primarily untrained new recruits. Second, Mexican morale problems are given more attention as a factor in the outcome.

The Conclusions explore the impact of the Béxar campaign on the strategy and tactics of Santa Anna, Fannin, and Travis in the spring of 1836, as well as its influence on leadership in the republic and state of Texas.

I wish to express my appreciation to Paul D. Lack, who offered thoughtful suggestions at several stages in the development of this study and read the entire manuscript. For their assistance I also wish to thank Yolanda Romero, Jodella Kite, Kenneth Kesselus, the staff of the Southwest Collection at

Texas Tech University, Don Carleton and the staff of the Barker
Texas History Center at the University of Texas at Austin,
Michael R. Green and other staff in the Archives Division of
the Texas State Library, Michael Hooks, Jesús F. de la Teja,
and the staff of the Archives of the Texas General Land Office,
the staff of the Daughters of the Republic of Texas Library at
the Alamo in San Antonio, and the readers and staff of the University of Texas Press.

The Alamo. From 31st Congress, 1st Session, Senate
Executive Document 32.

Martín Perfecto de Cos.

Edward Burleson. From Homer S. Thrall, Pictorial History of Texas, *p. 223.*

Erastus "Deaf" Smith. Courtesy San Jacinto Museum of History, Houston, Texas.

James Fannin. Courtesy Dallas Historical Society.

James Bowie. Courtesy Archives Division, Texas State Library.

Stephen F. Austin. Courtesy Texas Memorial Museum, acc. #1495.

William Barret Travis. Courtesy Archives Division, Texas State Library.

*Who Will Go with Old Ben Milam into San Antonio? by Henry A. McArdle.
Courtesy Daughters of the Republic of Texas Library at the Alamo, San Antonio.*

*Veramendi House. Courtesy Daughters of the Republic of Texas Library
at the Alamo, San Antonio.*

Concepción mission. From William Corner, San Antonio de Bexar, *following p. 8.*

San Fernando church. Courtesy Archives Division, Texas State Library.

TEXANS IN REVOLT
The Battle for San Antonio, 1835

ONE

INTRODUCTION

Anglo Americans under the leadership of Stephen F. Austin and other empresarios came to Texas in wagons and sailing ships in the 1820s to seek land.[1] Mexican government leaders authorized the immigration as a means of populating their northeastern frontier region and making it more productive. The settlers agreed to accept Mexican laws, including the state-supported Roman Catholic church, yet their location on the frontier left them generally untouched by the authority of the Mexican government.

Historians seeking causes for later unrest have at times pointed to the religious requirement, lack of public education, problems of frontier protection, or limits on immigration. Yet none of these issues appears significant. Small groups of settlers occasionally held Protestant religious services, while some worshiped on a family basis and others ignored religion entirely—patterns common to frontier areas in the United States. State-supported education did not develop in the United States until the 1830s in New England and did not spread effectively across the South until the 1850s or even after the Civil War. Parents taught children in the home or with the aid of a few private teachers in Texas, as in other newly settled regions. Conflict with Indians over control of territory flared in Texas as on the United States frontier, with local militia providing much of the protection for settlements in both places. Mexican concern about United States interest in acquiring Texas and the growth

of Anglo population in the region led to a law in 1830 that officially halted immigration from the neighboring nation. Considerable illegal immigration continued, however, followed by a
relaxation of the limits in 1834.

More serious concerns among the Texan pioneers arose over
land claims, taxes, and the relationships between local, state,
and national governments in Mexico. The earliest conflict over
land claims developed in the Nacogdoches area of East Texas
between old Mexican settlers and newly arrived Anglos. Haden
Edwards stirred the brief and unsuccessful Fredonian Rebellion
in 1826, which met opposition from Austin as well as Mexican
authorities. Frustrations concerning the government grew in
the 1830s, however, over slow issuance of land titles. Disagreement between the state and national governments over land
grants to speculators in the mid-1830s left Texans divided, with
some irritation directed at the government and some at the persons who had promoted the grants.

The collection of new trade taxes in the 1830s led to protests
and fighting. Texans had been exempt from taxes collected in
other parts of Mexico as an added attraction for new immigrants
in the 1820s. When Mexico tried to collect the customs duties
in the 1830s, the change, along with inconsistencies by local
officials, led to harassment of the officers and arrests of the pro-
testors at Anahuac. A battle followed at Velasco in 1832. The
military overthrow of the Mexican president by General Antonio
López de Santa Anna relieved tension, since he announced in
favor of federalism and the exercise of more local authority. Appeals for increased local government in Texas by unofficial con-
ventions in 1832 and 1833 struck a responsive chord, when in
1834 the Mexican government created the department of Béxar,
which included the Texas settlements. Six of these communities
received designation as municipalities, while representation
from Texas in the state legislature also increased.

When Santa Anna reversed his position to support a stronger
central government in 1834 and 1835, he responded to the economic and political problems of a new nation, not unlike those
of the Confederation period in the 1780s that had led to a

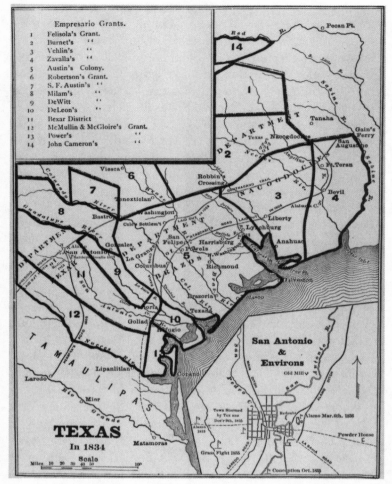

1. Texas in 1834. From Homer S. Thrall, Pictorial History of Texas *(St. Louis: N. D. Thompson and Company, 1879), following p. 168.*

stronger central government in the United States under the Constitution in 1787. Yet Santa Anna's military approach revived fears among Texans about several issues. Renewed but uneven efforts to collect customs duties led to new clashes at Anahuac in June 1835. The reduction in power for state governments brought concern about a loss of recent local and state au-

3

thority. A stronger central government might decide to enforce in Texas the Law of 1829, which abolished slavery, an action that would undermine the developing use of slave labor in the frontier region. An undercurrent of cultural and racial differences fed the growing unrest. Mexican leaders feared the aggressive influence of the United States in each new outbreak of protest. Older immigrants to Texas had assimilated Mexican culture in many ways over the span of a decade. New settlers in the 1830s often had lived entirely within growing Anglo colonies, however, and had made few adjustments to the Spanish traditions of Mexico. Many tended to view as inferior a people of both Spanish and Indian ancestry.

In 1835 Santa Anna released Austin from prison, where he had spent several months for proposing creation of a state government in Texas without approval from Mexican authorities. To halt the recent protests in Texas, however, the Mexican leader ordered new arrests of several outspoken critics. A growing number of Anglo Texans rallied to oppose such action, encouraged by similar resistance in other Mexican states, including Zacatecas.

To protect his position in San Antonio de Béxar and to limit further threats, Colonel Domingo de Ugartechea in September 1835 called upon the alcalde at Gonzales to return a cannon provided earlier for defense against Indians. When the settlers did not comply, the Mexican commander sent a company of cavalry for the artillery piece. Anglo Texans from nearby communities hurried to the support of Gonzales. On October 2, 1835, the two forces faced each other along the Guadalupe River as a morning fog cleared. The Texans refused to surrender the cannon and opened fire. Following a brief exchange of shots, the Mexican soldiers withdrew toward Béxar. Protest had become open resistance. To leaders on both sides, the key to the immediate future could only be the government and military headquarters for the entire region, San Antonio de Béxar.

TWO

TWO ARMIES

Soldiers gathered in groups on an early fall morning to listen to appeals from candidates for commander in chief, and spokesmen moved about the camp in the Guadalupe River valley to urge support for the leading figure from their region. Ambitious officers sought a higher position, yet none had a reputation that extended beyond his own settlement. Excited voices rose in disagreement, and threats flew that men would depart if their choice failed to achieve a majority in the voting scheduled for four o'clock that afternoon, October 11, 1835. A military command seemed to be on the verge of disintegration. Had it been a peacetime militia muster, it might have produced another colorful example of frontier humor in nineteenth-century American literature. But these volunteers formed the Texan army which had just defended Gonzales and its cannon from Mexican troops at the beginning of October.

While new recruits had arrived each day, about a hundred men had rushed off to defend settlers around Victoria from a reported Mexican force. A message from Colonel Domingo de Ugartechea had arrived four days earlier urging peace, but warning that the alternative would be a new advance from San Antonio. Faced with an urgent need for leadership and coordination, delegates from the various companies formed a war council. After three days of decisions by committee, the group authorized the election of a commander. Yet even that plan had proved divisive. If some of the men scattered back to their farms, even temporarily, resistance in Texas to centralization of power throughout Mexico by President Antonio López de Santa Anna might collapse.[1]

Early in the afternoon a "slender . . . graceful" man "with . . . dark hair . . . hazel eyes" and a "magnetic" personality rode into the camp. The soldiers began to cheer when they recognized Stephen F. Austin. As the leader of Anglo colonization in Texas since the early 1820s, Austin remained the best-known figure among those settlers. After years of cooperation with the Mexican government and efforts to solve differences between colonists and national authorities, he had been jailed in Mexico City during 1834 for proposing improper action in an injudicious moment. He returned to Texas after his release in the summer of 1835 determined to oppose the concentration of power by Santa Anna, a decision that unified most sentiment in the Anglo settlements in favor of resistance. In the early fall Austin had promoted the creation of a Texas governing body and the gathering of men and supplies to defend Gonzales and other communities from possible occupation. Several military leaders at Gonzales urged him to forward supplies and to join them to confer about decisions. His nephew, Moses Austin Bryan, worried because Austin "was so feeble that his servant Simon had to assist him to mount his horse" as he hurried forward to join the army. When Austin arrived, John A. Wharton immediately nominated him for commander in chief, arguing, "Austin can come nearer uniting the people than any other man, and, furthermore, it will give us better standing abroad." Other candidates agreed and withdrew as the volunteers came together again in support of Austin to lead "the Army of the People."[2]

Austin provided the solution to the leadership crisis, but he faced a new challenge at Gonzales. With little military experience, he had the task of organizing the short-term, democratic volunteers into a fighting force that could take the offensive. "But one spirit and one purpose animates the people of this part of the country," explained Austin, "and that is to take

Bexar, and drive the Military out of Texas. . . . A combined effort of all Texas would soon free our soil of Military despots— we should then have peace, for the present Gov of Mexico have too much to do at home . . . to send another army to Texas."[3]

Austin had proved himself as a political leader, first in the Missouri territorial legislature beginning in 1814 and then as the most successful empresario in Texas during the 1820s and 1830s. Yet he had led only two brief forays against Indian raiders in Texas and the militia of his colony in opposing the Fredonian Rebellion. Each incident had been settled peacefully by Austin, who exhibited the talents of a diplomat more clearly than those of a soldier. His creation of militia for frontier protection, however, had provided him with some insight into the organizational needs of the Texan army in 1835.[4]

The first step in creating a military structure became the election of regimental officers. For colonel the men selected John H. Moore of La Grange, an experienced Indian fighter who had successfully led the defense of Gonzales ten days earlier. The volunteers chose as lieutenant colonel Edward Burleson, a former militia officer in Missouri and Tennessee. Finally, the position of major went to Alexander Somervell, a merchant from Brazoria.[5]

The new commander immediately issued orders for an inspection the next morning in preparation for an advance on San Antonio. He banned any unauthorized firing of weapons, provided for guards around the army and its animals, and warned his men that "patriotism and firmness will avail but little, without discipline and strict obedience to orders." To strengthen and maintain his troops, Austin called on the Committee of Safety at San Felipe for reinforcements, ammunition, and food. Even before his arrival, the volunteers had mounted the small Gonzales cannon on wheels made from slices of a tree trunk. Noah Smithwick, with experience as a gunsmith, directed the work, which also included hammering files to make lance tips and molding ammunition for rifles and shotguns. Since "we had neither swords nor bayonets and few of us had pistols," as Smithwick explained, they practiced having one group fire and then retreat for reloading while another unit took its place. Thus they hoped to hold off any rapid charge by Mexican cavalry.[6]

The three hundred volunteers who formed for Austin's inspection on October 12 represented the Anglo Texan colonies of Austin and Green DeWitt. When the first call for aid had gone out from Gonzales on September 25, Robert M. Coleman had responded by gathering about forty of his neighbors around Mina, or Bastrop. They had joined Albert Martin and his original eighteen Gonzales men just after dark on the twenty-ninth. From La Grange, farther down the Colorado River, had come forty more settlers led by John H. Moore. When Mathew Caldwell had arrived the next day from Washington-on-the-Brazos with another hastily collected company, the troops numbered 150 for the skirmish on October 2. Following the clash, four companies of additional recruits had hurried forward under James W. Fannin, Jr., and others. About half of the volunteers had immigrated to the Mexican border state during the 1820s and included members of Austin's Old Three Hundred settlers. Almost all of the others had entered Texas between 1830 and 1834. Most had come from the South, with only a scattering of northerners. The largest numbers hailed from Tennessee, Kentucky, Louisiana, and Virginia. Landowning farmers formed the bulk of the volunteers, with an occasional merchant, professional man, or skilled craftsman. Relatively young men in their twenties and thirties filled most of the ranks. A majority of the men had left wives and families at home as they rushed to join the army.[7]

The Texan volunteers lacked professional military training, yet several had served as militia in earlier campaigns. A few had fought in the War of 1812. James G. Swisher, who led a company from the Washington municipality in 1835, had been with the Tennessee militia and later the United States army between 1813 and 1815. At least a dozen of the volunteers had seen action at Velasco in 1832, when Texans had captured the Mexican fort and garrison in a bloody dispute over customs collection. Among the 112 Texan volunteers at Velasco, 34 had suffered wounds, of whom 7 had died. Yet the victors seemed to

8

have recalled more clearly that they had killed or disabled 50 among the 150 soldiers in the Mexican command. Valentine Bennet had recovered from two wounds at Velasco to become a lieutenant in 1835. Several volunteers had joined companies to counter Indian raids along the frontier. As late as July and August 1835, calls went out from Columbia for the creation of three militia companies to gather at Bastrop in August for that purpose. Robert M. Coleman had led a company of men from Bastrop against Indians twice that year. One participant suggested, however, that frontier defense could be used to disguise the organization of a force for opposing Mexican authority. Five of the volunteers had helped stop the collection of customs on the coast in June 1835. Andrew Briscoe and William Barret Travis had formed a company from around Harrisburg to capture the small Mexican garrison at Anahuac. Other militia units had been created at San Felipe and Bastrop during June and July. When Cos had come ashore with additional troops on the Texas coast in September, Anglo militia had gathered at settlements from Bastrop to Velasco. Austin and Branch T. Archer had urged the companies to meet near the Lavaca River to face Cos before he could reach Béxar. Calls for support from Gonzales had diverted most of those men to the confrontation over the cannon.

Most of the volunteers had a familiarity with firearms, at least for hunting. While the Texans lacked the discipline of regulars, many had experience which provided the potential for a successful fighting force. Service with southern militia in the Creek War of 1812–1814 frequently involved defense of forts or camps against Indian attack. Commanders like Andrew Jackson at Horseshoe Bend took the offensive when they had numerical superiority to go along with their firepower advantage from artillery and rifles. Typical tactics included encirclement and crossfire from cover followed by attack when the Indians began to waver. Against Mexican troops in 1832, Texan volunteers used similar tactics. At Velasco riflemen firing from the cover of scattered logs, a ship, and ditches had forced the surrender of Mexican soldiers who were defending a fort with muskets and a cannon. Texans at Nacogdoches occupied houses to avoid Mexican shots from the Old Stone Fort. Texan firepower drove off a cavalry advance. Harassing attacks by the Texans on retreating Mexican troops at creek and river fords led to Mexican surrender. In Texas, where mounted Indians represented more mobile adversaries, fighting usually involved defense of settlements or dismounted surprise counterattacks on Indian villages where the range and accuracy of rifles at up to three hundred yards provided an advantage. The Texan troops represented a strong volunteer military tradition that had developed on the southern frontier.[8]

Austin moved his men across the Guadalupe River on October 12 to a new encampment in preparation for an advance on San Antonio. To strengthen the army, he called on the officers who had captured Goliad to return with part of their men and captured ammunition to join him. He also urged the Committee of Safety at San Felipe to send forward reinforcements, especially those expected from Nacogdoches. Responses from the leaders at those points indicated little hope of aid from Goliad but offered the expectation of cannon and munitions from the United States which had been landed on the coast.[9]

Observations from two days in camp led Austin to issue further orders. He reminded the men to be constantly prepared for action, admonished those on watch against sleeping, and called for an end to "riotous conduct and noisy clamorous talk." Horses should not be left loose at night, and new recruits must join an organized company of at least thirty men and avoid straggling on the march.[10]

The Texas troops offered a striking sight as they left camp to take the road for Béxar. Noah Smithwick, one of the volunteers, explained that

> our only arms were Bowie knives and long single-barreled, muzzle-loading flintlock rifles . . . [though others mentioned shotguns]. Buckskin breeches were the nearest approach to uniform, . . . some being new and soft and yellow, while others, from long familiarity with rain and grease and dirt,

had become hard and black and shiny. . . . Boots being an
unknown quantity; some wore shoes and some moccasins.
Here a broad-brimmed sombrero overshadowed the military
cap at its side; there a tall "beegum" rode familiarly beside a
coonskin cap, with the tail hanging down behind. . . . Here
a big American horse loomed up above the nimble Spanish
pony ranged beside him; there a half-broke mustang pranced
beside a sober, methodical mule. Here a bulky roll of bed
quilts jostled a pair of "store" blankets; there the shaggy
brown buffalo robe contrasted with a gaily checkered counter-
pane. . . . In lieu of a canteen, each man carried a Spanish
gourd. . . . A fantastic military array to a casual ob-
server. . . . So with the Old Cannon flag flying at the head,
and the "artillery" flying at the heels of two yokes of long-
horned Texas steers occupying the post of honor in the center,
we filed out of Gonzales and took up the line of march for San
Antonio.[11]

The goal of the Texans, San Antonio de Béxar, lay in a gently
rolling valley on the west side of the spring-fed San Antonio
River. Stone buildings with thick walls surrounded two plazas
that were intersected by broad streets. Between the main plaza
nearer the river and the military plaza to the west stood a
church whose tower overlooked the community of perhaps six-
teen hundred people. West of the military plaza ran San Pedro
Creek. Beyond the rock houses lay scattered log and mud huts.
The river ran ninety feet wide but only a yard deep and formed
a horseshoe bend east of the town toward an abandoned and
crumbling Spanish mission, San Antonio de Valero. The mission had become known as the Alamo either because of cotton-
wood trees nearby or as a result of the Álamo company of soldiers which had been quartered there. To the south along the
river stood the ruins of four more missions that had been
founded over a hundred years before, as was the town, but had
been secularized in the 1790s with only their chapels used for
services. Above and below the town lay fertile fields of corn.
On September 16 the Bexareños had celebrated the indepen-

11

dence Mexico had won a decade earlier. Yet the predominantly Mexican Texan citizens found themselves in an awkward situation. Many shared Anglo Texan concerns about the centralization of political authority, but they worried about rumors of Anglo independence sentiment. Choosing sides in a civil war would be difficult enough without facing the possible changes brought by a revolution that would thrust them into minority status.[12]

On October 9, 1835, two days before Austin joined the Texan army at Gonzales, General Martín Perfecto de Cos, "a small but well-favored man of pure Castillian blood," entered San Antonio to assume direction of Mexican forces in Texas. He had commanded the Eastern Interior Provinces since his appointment in September 1834 by President Santa Anna, his brother-in-law. Cos had faced scattered unrest across northern Mexico that had kept him and a majority of his limited forces in Coahuila and Tamaulipas during the spring of 1835. His ranking officer in Texas, Colonel Domingo de Ugartechea, had opposed the Texans at Velasco in 1832 and had won their respect as "a stranger to fear." Yet he had found himself beset by lack of funds, supplies, horses, and men into the summer of 1835. In late June, Ugartechea had commanded four companies or detachments in Texas with about 200 men on their rolls, but only 100 had been concentrated at Béxar, Goliad, and Anahuac to control the Indian frontier, customs collection, and political unrest. Cos had considered sending the Morelos Battalion of infantry to Texas as early as February, but he had been unable to forward the unit until July. The battalion had reached Béxar with only 143 men and officers. During the same month, following the Texan capture of the small Anahuac garrison, Ugartechea finally had received three new cavalry companies, which had brought the mounted force at Béxar to 364 men, though only about half were available for active duty. Between 50 and 100 infantry and artillerymen also had been brought in by the end of September.[13]

Cos had arrived by sea at Copano Bay on September 21 with cavalrymen from several units, had advanced by the twenty-eighth to the Mexican post at Lipantitlán, on the Nueces River, and on October 1 reached the small garrison at Goliad. When he arrived in San Antonio to join Ugartechea, their combined forces numbered 647 men ready for duty. Referring to the 200 infantry in the Morelos Battalion, led by Colonel Nicolás Condelle, an Anglo resident of Béxar reflected his military and racial views by pronouncing them "the best soldiers in the Republic (of the Mexican breed.)" The infantry with some artillery held the plazas west of the river, while the remaining cannoneers garrisoned the Álamo east of the river with over 400 cavalry in seven companies—one each from Béxar, Álamo de Parras, Tamaulipas, Agua Verde, Río Grande, and two from Nuevo León. At the San Antonio church on Sunday, October 11, Cos and his men celebrated mass, for which they provided martial music. The same day Cos learned that the Texans had seized Goliad, which cut his line of communication with the coast. Because the Mexican general believed that Béxar would be the primary goal of the Texans, he decided to keep his limited force united to defend that post.[14]

The San Antonio garrison reflected the strengths and weaknesses of the Mexican army, which had emerged from over a decade of revolution, 1810–1823, to face new peacetime problems. In the 1820s the Mexican military included long-time revolutionaries and last-minute converts from the Spanish army, though the number of Spanish officers declined as a result of opposition to their continuation in positions of leadership. Financial difficulties and political conflicts hurt military discipline and forced a reduction in the size of the army. The government concentrated the largest contingents near Gulf ports to guard against renewed Spanish interest or along the northern Indian frontier.[15]

The Mexican army had suffered losses and disruption in the civil wars of the 1830s. New soldiers had been drafted from workers in towns, peasants on farms, and some prisoners in jails. Anglo Texans spoke of "convict" soldiers, although such replacement troops may have been similar in some ways to the indentured servants in the English colonies. One Anglo Texan described part of the Morelos Battalion in September as "a Colonel Commandant . . . Four Lieut. Cols. two of which appear to be gentlemen and Captains by the dozen and Lieutenants by the scores and from that down to negroes, one of which is a first Sergent to one of the Companies." The observer believed the imbalance between an excessive number of officers and a limited number of enlisted men resulted from desertion. Certainly these regular army infantry found themselves far from their homes in central Mexico, but that background probably gave them a stronger commitment to the national government. The presidial cavalry, more like militia, served in their own border region, which reflected greater discontent with the central government. Yet these troops from northern Mexico had experience in hunting and frontier conditions which gave them military potential. The ethnic diversity of the Mexican army also could be a source of strength. While men of Spanish ancestry held more officers' positions, men of Indian and black ancestry could advance their social status through successful military service.[16]

Arms in the Mexican army included lances, swords, and old British muskets for the cavalry. Infantry carried muskets and some British rifles and bayonets. The muskets lost accuracy between fifty and one hundred yards, while the rifles might hit a target at twice that range. The strong recoil of these weapons further reduced their accuracy. The soldiers received training in tactics based on the Napoleonic Wars, as did the United States army and most of its European counterparts. Those tactics involved short-range volley firing followed by bayonet attacks, supported by cavalry armed with lances or sabers. Uniforms ranged from blue pants and red or blue jackets to white cotton pants and shirts, and Anglo Texans sometimes referred to Mexican troops in San Antonio as the "bluecoats." Officers added colorful epaulets and sashes. The closing phrase common to official army correspondence, "God and Liberty," provided a reminder that the Mexican army also represented a revolutionary tradition still vivid in the thinking of many of its officers and men, even as they stood in the path of a new rebellion.[17]

THREE

ADVANCE TO CONCEPCIÓN

S tephen F. Austin led his men
west on October 13, 1835, out of Gonzales in the direction of
San Antonio. When the Anglo Texans advanced beyond the
heavily wooded Guadalupe River valley with its tall trees, they
left the East and Central Texas environment of their settlements. As they marched across rolling redland prairies with
grass and scattered oak clusters, they emerged into a South
Texas landscape where they felt less comfortable and more exposed to attack by Mexican cavalry. Thus the army proceeded
at a rate of only about ten miles each day.

To help grapple with the new setting, Austin gained the aid
of Ben Milam, a former empresario who joined the command
on the fourteenth after escaping arrest at Saltillo and assisting in
the capture of Goliad. Austin assigned Milam to direct a company of scouts in gathering information about the Mexican army
at Béxar. To protect against surprise attack, Austin the next day
ordered the troops to camp facing outward around their horses
in the middle. When its makeshift carriage failed by a small
creek, the Texans left the Gonzales cannon, whose value had
been primarily symbolic. The small fieldpiece had been spiked
and buried, then renovated. Thus firing it might have proved
difficult, with distance and accuracy problematical; it probably
could have been effective only at close range when loaded with
scrap metal.[1]

When the Texans reached Cibolo Creek on October 16,

scouts made contact with Mexican patrols. Austin called a halt to await additional troops. Perhaps he also felt some concern as a result of advice from his friend William H. Jack that an assault on San Antonio faced unfavorable odds. The next day the Texan commander directed a message to General Cos during a truce, offering to negotiate differences and to allow for peace in the province. In response Cos sought a middle ground, refusing to recognize the colonists except through petition and calling on Austin to disband his force. Yet Cos also expressed a reluctance to initiate armed conflict. Ugartechea sent cavalry to reconnoiter the Texan force during the seventeenth. Texan guards and pickets ranged out to gather information and to detect any Mexican movements. An early Texan foray to surprise a Mexican squad that defended a ford on Salado Creek had resulted in suspense, jumpy reactions to night sounds, and a whispered debate over the situation. The absence of Mexican troops brought relief and even laughter over their false worries.[2]

The Texan officers, in consultation with their commander on the eighteenth, argued that they should remain on the Cibolo. Austin placed four companies on alert, however, for an advance on short notice. A second officers' meeting the following day took a more aggressive stand, based on the arrival of three new companies led by John Bird, Jacob Eberly, and James C. Neill, who commanded two new six-pounder cannon. This brought the army strength to 453, though illness and detachments reduced the available troops to 384. Austin then ordered an advance to Salado Creek on October 20. At the same time, the Texas commander again sent for artillery to strengthen the firepower of his force.[3]

When his patrols informed Cos of the Texans approaching San Antonio, he immediately began to strengthen the defenses of both the town and the Alamo mission across the river. Anglo and Mexican Texans in Béxar received orders to assist in these efforts. Mexican troops dug ditches, erected log and earth barricades across the roads opening into the two plazas, and positioned four cannon for action by October 17. Ammunition was stored in the church. Work continued at a rapid pace, which resulted by October 26 in fortifications that bristled with eleven light cannon: five to defend corners of the town squares and six on the walls of the mission, as well as an eighteen-pounder positioned in the Alamo chapel for greater range. Cos warned his men against appeals from the Texans and encouraged the Mexican soldiers to achieve glory through valor and defense of "the national interests." To keep information from the approaching Texans, he began to control movement in and out of the town, though messages continued to slip through from civilians. A comet in the sky attracted notice and speculation about whether it symbolized success for one army or the other.[4]

During the march across the prairie from the Cibolo to the Salado, the Texan army gained new recruits with valuable insights because of their background. James Bowie arrived from San Antonio, his home since 1830. His varied career as a slave trader, knife fighter, dealer in land and mining, veteran of the battle at Nacogdoches in 1832, and member by marriage of the prominent Veramendi family in San Antonio made him attractive as a man familiar with Mexican society as well as with conflict. He had drunk heavily after his wife died of cholera in 1833, but the forty-year-old Bowie still seemed an imposing figure as a six-footer with a serious demeanor. Erastus ("Deaf") Smith of Béxar found his return home from a hunting trip blocked forcefully by Mexican soldiers and fled on a fast horse amid an exchange of gunfire. He was sturdy, red headed, and something of a loner because he had been born with limited hearing. Born in New York during 1787, he had moved to Mississippi and then to San Antonio, where he had married a Mexican widow. Still angry from his reception by Mexican troops, he galloped into the Texan camp. "General Austin," said Smith, "I told you yesterday that I would not take sides in this war but, Sir, I now tender you my services as the Mexicans acted rescally with me." With him came Hendrick Arnold, a free black man and fellow hunter who had wed the daughter of Smith's wife by her first husband. All three men brought word of Cos' defense measures and of possible unrest among the Mexican cavalry, a view supported by a deserter from San Antonio.[5]

By October 22 the Texan army received important reinforcements when Juan N. Seguín, a government official from San Antonio and the son of Erasmo Seguín, a former alcalde of the community, rode into camp only five days before his twenty-ninth birthday. With him came a company of thirty-seven Mexican Texans, some of whom had served in a militia unit that had been disbanded by Ugartechea when it had supported the state government of Coahuila earlier in the year. The young alcalde for Victoria, Plácido Benavides, soon arrived from Goliad to add at least twenty-six soldiers to the new company, and in the days that followed, Salvador Flores and Manuel Leal brought over forty recruits from the ranches along the stream south of Béxar. Seguín and the other Mexican Texans, who grew to number 135, proclaimed themselves defenders of the Mexican Constitution of 1824, the official position of Austin and the Consultation organized at San Felipe that fall. Their presence broadened the base of Texan resistance to centralization of the Mexican government under Santa Anna. The Mexican Texans and Hendrick Arnold blurred the sense of ethnic conflict reflected in the comment at Gonzales by a Texan volunteer: "The Anglo-American spirit appears in every thing we do." Some Anglo volunteers probably felt suspicious of the new recruits, while others welcomed their support. Austin immediately sent Seguín to buy food from the Mexican Texans in the countryside around San Antonio to sustain the Texas troops.[6]

With his considerable reinforcements, Austin decided to probe closer to San Antonio. To lead the movement, he appointed James Bowie a colonel to jointly command "the first Division of the first Batallion" with Captain James W. Fannin, Jr. Fannin had resigned from the United States Military Academy after two years as a cadet from Georgia, yet that experience made him one of the few Texas officers with military training. After immigration to Texas during 1834, he had smuggled slaves into the region. When unrest developed in 1835, he spoke out for opposition to Santa Anna and hurried forward with a company to Gonzales. For a man of thirty-one with his background, conflict represented an opportunity to further his fortunes in a newly adopted homeland.[7]

Bowie and Fannin led their men across a rolling prairie through scattered mesquite growth toward the missions along the San Antonio River below the town on October 22. Austin directed them to establish friendly contacts with Mexican Texans in the area and to send back food for the troops. He also wanted them to locate the Mexican horse herds and to select one mission as a campsite that would control the road from Goliad. By late afternoon they had driven Mexican pickets from Espada mission and seized the buildings. From Mexican Texans they learned that Cos had improved the town defenses but had only limited supplies and that he kept his horses close to San Antonio. In the hope of a quick victory, Bowie and Fannin suggested that Austin camp north of the community, an action that would allow the two groups of Texans to close off all movement in and out of the town.[8]

The following day Bowie and Fannin reconnoitered San Juan and San José missions but found little food or water and withdrew to Espada for the night. They reported that a small body of Mexican troops had slipped into Béxar under cover of darkness. To purchase food they requested funds from Austin as well as an additional fifty men for patrol purposes. Austin responded by sending the soldiers, but he could only offer his personal promise of payment to possible suppliers of food. At the same time, he continued to urge the shipment of supplies from Goliad.[9]

Scouts for both armies had made occasional contact without casualties. Then on October 22 in the first skirmish, the Texans wounded two Mexican soldiers and killed another. Two days later in clashes near Salado Creek and Espada mission, Texan scouts drove off Mexican foragers who fell back with one killed and a few wounded. Yet Cos only awaited the arrival of reinforcements before striking back at the Texans. From the government of San Antonio, he requested mules to make his forces more mobile. Between October 22 and 24, the Mexican army grew in size. Over the three-day period, Cos received three groups of reinforcements that totaled 100 men. Cos also called for and received some volunteers from Béxar. Thus the Mexican forces probably peaked on October 24 at over 751 men.[10]

Abruptly the focus of attention in the Texan army shifted from questions of encircling or attacking San Antonio to political issues. The Consultation had been called to meet in San Felipe de Austin for the purpose of establishing an official position for Texas toward the Mexican government, as well as a permanent body to coordinate military and civilian activities. Some soldiers had been chosen as delegates to the meetings, but other volunteers resented their departure from the fighting front at a time when supplies had dwindled. Grumbling spread through the ranks as many men spoke of going home.

To resolve the sudden crisis, Austin called for a discussion of the question before the entire command on October 25. Among the speakers stood Sam Houston, who recently had arrived in camp "mounted on a little yellow Spanish stallion so diminutive that old Sam's long legs, incased in the conventional buckskin, almost touched the ground." Despite his lack of service with the army, he received a hearing because of his past experience in both war and politics. He had been wounded by Creek Indians during the battle of Horseshoe Bend in 1814, which resulted in his appointment as a lieutenant by General Andrew Jackson. After the War of 1812, Houston had become a lawyer and political figure in Tennessee, serving as a congressman and as governor in the 1820s before the failure of his marriage led to his resignation and exile among the Cherokee Indians. Business interests and Indian affairs had led him to Texas, where he finally settled in Nacogdoches by 1835. He had been active in resistance meetings that fall and now visited the army as a delegate to the Consultation. At forty-two Houston remained an imposing figure, over six feet in height but aging in appearance after an active life that included drinking bouts in moments of depression. Yet as Houston stepped forward to address the soldiers, his prospects, and possibly ambitions, seemed to be on

the rise after his recent appointment to lead the soldiers raised
in Nacogdoches. He spoke enthusiastically for the Consultation, but opposed an attack on San Antonio until the soldiers
received further training and more cannon. If the volunteers
accepted his views, the campaign might end with the army following Houston eastward.[11]

Branch T. Archer also spoke, followed by William H. Jack.
Austin concluded the speeches despite illness which left him
"just able to sit on his horse." Each speaker favored unity and
urged that representatives be sent to the Consultation. Austin
further proposed continued pressure on the Mexican forces in
San Antonio "as long as 10 men would stick to him." Most volunteers again rallied to Austin's support, while allowing a number of delegates including Houston to leave for the Consultation. Rebuffed in his military advice, Houston on October 28
reached Gonzales, where he met men hauling cannon to the
army at San Antonio. Again he counseled against an assault
on the Mexican-held town and tried unsuccessfully to convince
the troops of his own views. To at least some of the soldiers,
he appeared "a vain, ambitious, envious, disappointed, dis-
contented man."[12]

On October 26 Austin turned his attention again to the Mexican army in San Antonio. He ordered his force of about four
hundred men to march toward the missions on the river below the town. Cos led over two hundred cavalry out to probe
for the Texans that day, but missed them and returned to Béxar.
At the close of the day, Austin learned of the Mexican movement by secret message from sympathizers in San Antonio. Unaware of their withdrawal, the Texan commander prepared to
meet a possible dawn assault by directing Burleson with one
hundred men to form under cover where they could watch for
an advance from town. Austin aroused the rest of his men in the
early hours and placed them to defend his camp. He hoped to
ambush the Mexican soldiers between the two wings of the
Texan army. Nervous anticipation increased with the morning
light. Then word came of a brief Mexican foray near Espada
mission to cover the arrival of a few new soldiers joining Cos.[13]

Austin rejoined the other wing of the army at Espada mission on October 27. He then sent Bowie and Fannin with their command forward to find a good defensive position which the entire force could occupy that evening. Austin also wanted information about the south side of San Antonio. Would an attack cross open ground or find cover? The general already had offensive plans in mind for his army. To protect against a counterthrust, Austin also established stronger guidelines for camp guards.[14]

Bowie and Fannin led ninety soldiers in four companies under Captains Andrew Briscoe, Robert Coleman, Michael Goheen, and Valentine Bennet. They moved north along the San Antonio River, passing the missions San Juan and San José. Mexican scouts skirmished briefly with the Texans and returned to inform Cos of the advance. When Bowie and Fannin approached the mission Concepción, they found an attractive campsite one-quarter mile to the west where the river curved in a horseshoe shape away from the mission. Trees shaded both sides of the broad riverbottom which lay about six feet below the level of the rolling prairie nearby. In the late afternoon, the two Texan commanders agreed to hold the site while a staff officer returned to the army to report their decision. Austin had expected them to return, however, instead of dividing the army with Mexican forces so close. Worry about the advanced division kept him awake while his men slept. The next day he issued a strong reminder that officers who failed to follow orders would be removed and courtmartialed.

Unaware of Austin's irritation, Bowie placed Fannin's men along the southern part of the horseshoe bend and personally positioned the other companies on the northern portion of the same curve in the river. Bowie posted pickets to sound an alarm if anyone approached during the night and assigned other guards to observe the area from the mission tower. As Noah Smithwick and the rest of Bowie's men bedded down for the night, they received an ominous reminder of their situation. "We were startled by a dull boom and . . . a cannon ball, shot from a gun mounted in the church tower two miles away, shrieked through the air overhead and buried itself in the earth

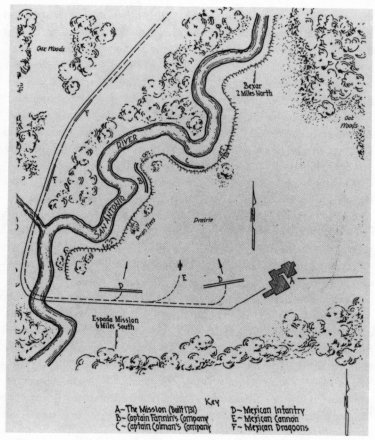

2. Battle of Concepción. Adapted from Andrew Jackson Houston, Texas
Independence *(Houston: Anson Jones Press, 1938), in pocket at back.*

a few rods beyond our camp. With a horrible hiss . . . another,
and another followed, to the number of half a dozen; then all
was still."[15]

Morning light came slowly on October 28 because of fog. Despite the limited visibility, Cos decided to move on the Texan
position, hoping to attack the advanced party before the main
body arrived. Colonel Domingo de Ugartechea led about 275
Mexican troops with two cannon out of San Antonio and down

the river at 6:00 A.M. Between 7:30 and 8:00 A.M., Mexican cavalry scouts suddenly loomed through the fog before one of the Texan pickets, Henry Karnes, and shot at him. He fired back, halting their advance, and then fell back to his company yelling, "Boys look out, its Karnes." When he tried to reload, Karnes shouted in frustration, "The d——d rascals have shot out the bottom of my powder-horn!" A second picket escaped serious injury when a bullet hit the knife that he had slipped through the front of his belt. The force of the shot left him temporarily disabled with an unusual wound.[16]

Slightly more than two hundred Mexican cavalry under Rafael Ugartechea held the west bank of the river, while Lieutenant Colonel Don José María Mendosa found a shallow place below the Texan position and led the infantry and artillery across the stream. To improve their field of vision, the Texans cut down undergrowth and dug out firing steps in the embankment from which they could drop down to reload. Light skirmishing lasted about two hours, then the fog thinned, and fifty to sixty Mexican infantry and artillery advanced across the prairie to complete the encirclement of the Texans. With the tree-lined riverbottom behind them, the Texans focused their attention on the approaching Mexican foot soldiers. Bowie shouted to his men, "Keep under cover, boys, and reserve your fire; we haven't a man to spare." The Texans crouched below the bank as "grape and canister crashed through the pecan trees overhead."[17]

When the Mexican infantry reached a point roughly three hundred yards away, they halted and spread into a line with the cannon in the center. The crackle of rifle fire sounded as the Texans began to snipe at the Mexican line with some accuracy from the edge of the bluff. The Mexican troops responded with crashing volleys that seemed a "continued blaze of fire," but also passed over the well-protected Texans. Mexican officers then ordered a charge on Fannin's line, and Bowie responded by bringing Coleman's company to reinforce the point of attack. While most of the Texans stayed below the bank as they shifted position, some rushed across the prairie. Among them Richard

Andrews fell wounded. When Smithwick lifted him and asked, "Dick, are you hurt?" he answered: "Yes, Smith, I'm killed." Increased fire from the Texans drove back the charge. The riflemen then turned their attention to the artillerymen who had advanced the cannon to within a hundred yards of the riverbank. Mexican cannoneers fell back with the infantry, leaving behind several dead. Again and again the Mexican officers rallied their infantry to renew the attack while the artillerymen returned to reload and discharge their cannon. Each time, the Texans broke the charge with rifle fire and then crept along the riverbank closer to the cannon. After the third assault had been turned away and the cannon stood silent amid dead cannoneers, a Mexican bugle sounded retreat. The few remaining infantrymen fell back across the river to get beyond rifle range, while the cavalry brought off the wounded and the artillery caisson. The Texans rushed forward yelling, "The cannon and victory," and swung the gun around to fire one parting shot. Another Mexican cannon with their cavalry replied twice to cover the withdrawal. Texan cavalry galloped onto the field at that moment and tried without success to overtake the Mexicans. The intense period of combat had lasted about thirty minutes.[18]

Austin and the remaining troops joined Bowie's command within half an hour after the fighting ended. The army had been up and preparing to advance before dawn. When a company left for home without authorization, however, a large body of guards unsuccessfully attempted to bring the men back. That wait, followed by problems hauling artillery and wagons across the river, slowed the advance. Yet Austin reached the battle-field in time to see the Mexican rear guard disappearing toward San Antonio. To his staff he exclaimed, "The army must follow them right into town" while Mexican morale remained low. Bowie and his officers immediately argued against the proposal. Austin consulted with his other officers, who agreed that without heavy artillery the fortifications of Béxar could not be stormed. With considerable disappointment and a sense of lost opportunity, Austin accepted that judgment. Later in the day, he allowed a priest and men from San Antonio to gather the bodies of the Mexican dead and to carry them off in carts.[19]

The Texan victory at Concepción resulted from able leadership, a strong position, and greater firepower. Smithwick described Bowie as "a born leader; never needlessly spending a bullet or imperiling a life." His selection of the riverbank defense line provided excellent protection from Mexican fire, and with their greater range, the Texan rifles proved highly effective at driving off each attack. Bowie had suffered only one killed and one wounded.[20]

The Mexican defeat at Concepción forced Cos to rethink his strategy and tactics. He had hoped to take advantage of the division in Texan troops to cut off and capture the smaller force. Yet the wooded riverbottom terrain had neutralized his cavalry, which never seriously joined the fray. A formal infantry assault with close artillery support over open ground had failed against a good defensive position and superior firepower. Mexican casualties included at least fourteen killed and thirty-nine wounded, but several of the wounded died later, and the total loss may have been sixty. The infantry bore the burden of the battle, for the cavalry lost only one killed and four wounded. Cos would avoid offensive action in the future.[21]

FOUR

ENCIRCLEMENT

Austin faced a dilemma after the victory at Concepción. Cos refused to sally forth from his fortified position in San Antonio, and the Texan officers generally opposed an attack upon those defenses. Thus Austin pursued several alternate ways to weaken the Mexican hold on Béxar.

On October 28, soon after the fighting ended at Concepción, Austin learned that about two hundred troops from Nacogdoches were approaching. He ordered them to pass close to the town on their way to his camp. Cos seemed unlikely to attempt another attack, while the fresh soldiers for the Texan army would further demoralize the Mexican forces. These volunteers from the East Texas settlements included several veterans of the 1832 skirmish at Nacogdoches, and some had joined militia companies raised in March and again in July 1835. At the head of the East Texans rode Thomas J. Rusk, the thirty-one-year-old son of an Irish immigrant to South Carolina. Seeking a defaulting debtor, Rusk had migrated at the end of 1834 to Nacogdoches, where he quickly became an active lawyer and political leader. The red-haired, well-built six-footer added a striking figure to the Texan officer corps. The arrival of the "Redlanders" brought the Texan army to a strength of six hundred, roughly comparable to that of Cos. From Goliad, Austin received twelve supply wagons carrying flour, salt, coffee, sugar, and liquor as well as soap, candles, tobacco, and cooking and eating utensils. Three light artillery pieces arrived early in November. With a larger and better supplied command, Austin felt prepared to pressure Cos.[1]

The Texan commander split his forces to threaten San Antonio from two directions. Bowie and Fannin held their position near the missions south of Béxar with four companies, while Austin and Moore led the rest of the army around to the river north of San Antonio on October 31. That day Bowie, acting autonomously, offered to discuss with Cos a peaceful solution to the confrontation. The Texan hinted that the Mexican commander could expect only further casualties and defeat if he did not respond. Messages from town led Austin to believe that two of the Mexican mounted companies might change sides if offered the right opportunity. Thus he ordered Bowie to skirmish with the outposts below town to provide the cavalrymen an excuse for leaving Béxar. Bowie and Fannin advanced to within half a mile of San Antonio on November 1 and held their ground, but no Mexican soldiers came to join them. To maintain their position, they urged Austin to provide additional men. The Texan commander officially called upon Cos to surrender that day, but the Mexican general refused to accept any message until the Texans laid down their weapons. Through the local priest, Cos later explained that his orders allowed him no choice except to resist any attack. Mexican artillery in the Alamo then exchanged fire with the Texan cannoneers, which confirmed the continued confrontation.[2]

To determine a course of action for his own forces, Austin called a "council of war" with all staff, regimental, and company officers in the northern wing early on November 2, 1835. Twenty-six men gathered to consider the possibility of an assault by the enlarged army or the alternative of harassing tactics until heavier artillery and more men arrived. Major Benjamin Smith argued for an attack, but lost to the more cautious counsel of the other officers. Bowie presented that decision to his officers of the southern wing in the afternoon. They agreed by a margin of nineteen to two. These officers then voted fourteen to seven in favor of joining Austin's command north of town.

Bowie viewed the second decision as a reflection of such unrest that he resigned as division commander. Austin accepted the recommendation expressed in the vote and ordered the southern unit to join the troops above San Antonio, who had established their camp at an old sugarcane mill near the river. Based upon the consensus decision, Austin sent staff officers to hurry forward heavy artillery and ammunition, which had been brought through Gonzales but had not reached Cibolo Creek.[3]

After the decision against an assault on Béxar, Texan troops who had been with the army since the Gonzales fight began to grow restless. Many men had been away from their families for a month or more. With the weather growing colder, soldiers who became ill found the army had little medicine for treating their problems. Men began to depart, some through official leave and others by their own choice. Individuals spoke of "going after that cannon" to excuse their absence. Others promised to return with the heavier clothes and equipment necessary for living outdoors in the winter. By November 4 Austin found his troops had dwindled to 450 and wrote in some despair to Branch T. Archer, president of the Consultation, about his "undisciplined militia" which, despite its success to that point, remained "in some respects of very discordant materials." The arrival of 180 troops from East Texas on the fifth left the commander with mixed feelings because of complaints that some had looted homes, frightened women, and attacked men as they passed through Gonzales. To avoid further discipline problems, he urged "no whysky be sent . . . to the camp" and placed two men under arrest until a hearing could be held. His own physical condition remained poor, which contributed to his depression. Yet Moses Austin Bryan watched his uncle "rest his head in his hands and speak to me of his bodily pains, and raise that head to meet his officers as if no pain was there."[4]

In late October, Austin had directed Colonel John H. Moore to create a cavalry force armed with "double barrel shot guns and pistols." A mounted company of fifty to eighty soldiers received official status on the twenty-seventh, under the command of Lieutenant William Barret Travis. The tall, handsome twenty-six-year-old officer had been born in the sometimes violent South Carolina upcountry county of Edgefield. He reached maturity and studied law in Alabama. His youthful marriage collapsed after an angry clash with another man, which sent Travis off to Texas in 1831. His rash temper quickly involved him in the Anahuac confrontation with Mexican officials over tax collection in 1832. Thereafter he established a law practice at San Felipe in which he exhibited considerable talent and energy. Yet his impetuous personality led him in active pursuit of female companionship, which produced awkward medical complications as well as possible legal problems, since he had never divorced. The same enthusiastic style made him a leader in the war party that captured Mexican soldiers at Anahuac in another disagreement over customs collection in the summer of 1835. His combative and energetic reputation had made him a controversial figure in prewar political discussions. The same traits brought him a junior officer's position once war began. In early November he led his first foray in search of Mexican horses that were being grazed somewhere below Béxar. When he returned empty handed, his injured pride led him to renounce his new rank of captain.[5]

Austin sent cavalry out regularly on the south side of San Antonio to capture Mexican dispatches. The mounted men also hoped to drive off any troops coming from the Rio Grande to the support of Cos. If the Texas cavalry could not stop such a movement, they could at least warn Austin of its approach. Seguín with his company seized a letter which explained that Mexican troops, who could have been brought to Béxar, had been concentrated against the foray of Colonel José Antonio Mexía toward Matamoros and Tampico.[6]

To forestall Mexican counterefforts, several officers urged even tighter restrictions against Mexican Texans collecting food, unless they served the Texan cause. Some officers worried about visits by local residents who might provide information to Cos.[7]

"Dissatisfaction, . . . aspiring men" and the changing nature of the Texan army created a new crisis in early November.

Some officers expected Austin to lead unhappy troops back to the Anglo settlements, leaving Bowie to harass the Mexican forces. Instead, despite "feeble" health and a belief that a political role better suited his talents, Austin reorganized his command on November 6 and 7. To replace John H. Moore, the soldiers elected Edward Burleson as colonel for the regiment with 351 votes over J. W. E. Wallace, who had 83 supporters; James Fannin with 68; Frank Johnson, 10; and Jim Bowie, 5. The Mexican Texans, who may have been out scouting, apparently did not participate in the election. There seems to have been no regional pattern in the voting. In such a democratic army, familiarity stirred reluctance as Burleson, Fannin, and Johnson all failed to carry majorities in their own original units. In a second ballot, Philip A. Sublett, a political leader from San Augustine, became lieutenant colonel of the regiment with a solid block of 145 votes from the five new East Texas companies and 116 votes in the older units for a total of 261, compared to 150 votes for Alexander Somervell and 54 for Wallace. Following his two election defeats, Wallace took leave from the army. To recognize the East Texans more fully, Austin organized their companies into a battalion which selected as its major Boyd Irvin. Privately Austin tried to reassure William Wharton, who thought he had been unfairly criticized. Nevertheless, Wharton resigned his staff position. Austin also appointed Bowie as adjutant general and Rusk as aide-de-camp. These efforts calmed most unrest and allowed the commander to tighten the siege by moving his headquarters to the missions south of the town, while maintaining a division north of San Antonio to limit entrance and departure by Mexican forces.[8]

As part of the effort to restrict Mexican movements, William Austin led a cavalry company west of the town on patrol during the eighth. When one soldier died from a chance mishap, the Texans continued their scout while calling for aid to recover the dead man. Captain Manuel Barragán with a Mexican patrol of forty cavalry encountered the Texan troops sent for the body and swept down on them. The Texans made a stand in a ravine before withdrawing beyond the river. Additional troops arrived

on the Texan side, which caused the Mexicans to break off the
engagement and retire with seven horses and some equipment
they had captured. To celebrate their trophies, the Mexican
commander sounded the bell in the church tower.[9]

Another cavalry company, led by Captain Andrew Briscoe,
soon returned from a longer scout down to the Medina River in
search of new Mexican troops or messengers from the Rio
Grande as well as foragers from San Antonio. Travis, who had
accompanied Briscoe, remained near the trail to Laredo with
twelve soldiers to continue those efforts. New reports on the
ninth of possible assistance for the Béxar garrison, including
up to 500 men, caused Austin to counter with a unit of 150
mounted troops under Fannin. From a central position near the
Atascosa River, they were to seek out and halt the relief column. Austin sent a rider to find Travis so that his men could
cooperate with Fannin. From Camp Defiance north of San Antonio, Burleson reported the arrival on the twelfth of Captain
Byrd Lockhart's cavalry company, which had found no Mexican activity. Burleson then sent out 70 soldiers under Major
Alexander Somervell to aid Fannin.[10]

Unaware of the larger troop movements, Travis had stopped
at dusk near the Salinas ranch along the Atascosa River on November 8. At first light he explored toward the Rio Grande until he found signs that a large herd of horses had passed through
from San Antonio. Cos probably had sent out his spare mounts
because they were in weak condition for lack of enough forage.
The Texas company then tracked the horses and their guards to
a stream at least fifty miles from Béxar. Signs of a day-old campsite led Travis to advance more carefully as the day faded into
darkness. To avoid detection the Texans halted "without water
& without shelter from the cold or rain which was falling upon
us." Travis advanced quickly and led a mounted attack on the
awakening Mexicans along San Miguel Creek. Caught off guard,
five soldiers on foot offered no resistance, while two who were
already mounted galloped away. Travis and his men then herded
the three hundred horses and mules back toward Béxar, sev-
enty miles away. After covering half that distance by the four-

teenth, Travis divided his men at the San Antonio River and ordered some to drive the herd on to Gonzales. While loss of the horses did not represent a major setback for the Mexican army, their capture lifted Texan morale and Travis' reputation.[11]

Throughout the first two weeks of November, skirmishing continued around Béxar. The armies frequently exchanged cannon and small arms fire, with little harm to either side. The Texans sought unsuccessfully to draw Mexican troops out into the open by advancing forces of 40 to 190 men to less than one-quarter mile of the defenses. During one exchange of fire on the eleventh, Mexican troops thought they had been shot at by Anglo civilians in the town, and a captain appeared at the home of John W. Smith to accuse him and Samuel Maverick of the act. A Mexican Texan who lived nearby relieved the tension by claiming that he had fired at Texans outside the town. Maverick became outraged over the incident, although he privately carried on a regular correspondence with the Texan army. Ugartechea and Condelle argued over the affair until Cos intervened with the comment, "The times don't allow brother-officers to quarrel." The general gave orders for the protection of civilians. On the following day, November 12, Colonel Ugartechea at the head of a cavalry force evaded the Texans and marched south to guide Mexican reinforcements coming from the Rio Grande.

Austin also struggled with internal problems. The monotony of camp life dulled the enthusiasm of his men: some refused to follow orders or fell asleep on duty; some took food or horses before they could be properly assigned; and others continued to depart without approval. Such actions led to new guidelines for discipline, with mixed results at best.[12]

The Texan commander constantly kept men in the field to harass the Mexican lines of supply and communication. As Travis returned, Austin also recalled Fannin, but sent out Salvador Flores with a company of Mexican Texans on the fourteenth to set fire to grasslands along the Nueces River and to continue the scouting operations. The following day, when Austin learned that Ugartechea had departed, the Texan leader feared an attack on Travis and Fannin. Although faced with conflicting reports which left him uncertain, Austin immediately sent out Burleson to direct 130 or more troops in an effort to defeat Ugartechea regardless of his goal. In response to concerns expressed by the division above Béxar, Austin also agreed to reunite his forces at the mill north of San Antonio. Fannin arrived back at the army camp on the eighteenth after a sweep across the Medina River. He divided his forces, sending Lieutenant John York on a swing west with one company while his own troops checked the trails to the east as far as the Atascosa and the Frio rivers. Both commands failed to find Mexican forces. Burleson came back later to report that no contacts had been made.[13]

At this point in mid-November, Austin faced a confusing array of pressures, problems, and opportunities. Members of the civilian government corresponded with various officers in the army, seeking information and offering advice. Houston, as the newly chosen general in chief of a regular army, asked Fannin to become inspector general. While careful to warn Fannin against deserting the forces at San Antonio, Houston again expressed doubts about the campaign and suggested that the army go into winter camp at Gonzales or Goliad. Fannin responded that he hoped for a general's rank in the regular army. Because of "the panic already imbibed, touching a storm," he agreed a retreat might be best, though he still believed San Antonio could be captured by attack. The exchange led to Fannin's resignation from the volunteer army by November 22. Travis stayed a little longer, but he left the army by the end of November for similar reasons.[14] Another political leader complained that the Texans had "been badly conducted" and could have had more provisions "if your commander or his staff could see 2 inches from their noses and order supplies in time." Yet he urged that the army continue the siege.[15] Lieutenant Governor James Robinson presented a more favorable view of support, in letters to Rusk, and encouraged the army to "be firm . . . and a crown of laurels must decorate the brow of every warrior in the camp."[16] Austin and other officers continued to inform the political leaders of the strong military position, while calling for new troops because of departures and supplies to maintain the army. The new General Council responded by seeking provisions for the troops. Thus the Texan officers could be depressed, distracted, or determined as they pursued their duties.[17]

Enlisted men suffered their own frustrations with the lengthening siege and new northers which brought rain and temperatures in the low forties by November 20. Soldiers cooked or slept instead of falling in for company formations. Individual firing, gambling, and other distractions became more common in the Texas camp, as did desertion. Grain for the horses and beef for the soldiers became scarce, which led Austin to issue orders for the careful distribution of corn and meat. Five companies listed 60 men absent or ill out of 211 on their rolls in late November.[18]

Amid these problems and pressures, Austin found one source of hope in the steady trickle of deserters from the Béxar garrison. To further disrupt the Mexican army, Austin hoped to use Colonel José María Gonzales, who had at one time served with two of the cavalry units at San Antonio. As a federalist who opposed Santa Anna's assumption of more centralized authority, he might be able to promote unrest by appeals to his former troops. Yet the unfriendly attitude of some Anglo Texans toward Gonzales and other Mexican federalists when they arrived at Goliad worried Austin. He protested their treatment to the provisional government and urged that they be asked to aid in the struggle for San Antonio. Austin issued his own proclamation to the Mexican Texan citizens of the town, seeking their support for the federalist cause.[19]

Beyond Mexican morale problems, Austin found other reasons for optimism. Small companies or groups of Texans appeared to strengthen the army. United States volunteers approached from the coast and through East Texas. With these reinforcements Austin again planned an assault on Béxar for dawn of November 22. To cover the attack, he ordered construction of an artillery emplacement near the river about three hundred yards north from the Alamo under cover of darkness, despite cold which dropped to near freezing. When Cos awoke to the new position, he scouted the battery before opening a bombardment. The Texans replied with their advanced cannon despite continued low temperatures. Austin met with his troops late on the day before the attack, spoke some words of encouragement, and directed them to be in position for the advance at 3:00 A.M. Finally the moment had arrived; the Texans would attempt to seize San Antonio. Then at 1:00 A.M. Lieutenant Colonel Philip Sublett awakened Austin. To his consternation the commander learned that most officers of one division thought the assault would fail and wanted to call it off. Austin quickly called Burleson, leader of the other division, to learn the views of those troops. To his surprise Austin found less than two hundred men, including the new United States volunteers, who still favored the assault. Frustration mixed with despair for Austin as he ordered the troops back to their camps.[20]

Austin and his staff believed that some individuals, "from motives of ambition and jealousy," had undermined his plan. A few days later staff members came to the conclusion that William H. Wharton, a former judge advocate of the army, had privately criticized each of Austin's attack proposals. They believed the purpose of Wharton's acts had been to leave the opportunity for victory to his friend Sam Houston. The staff officers also learned of Houston's missives to officers in which he argued against the campaign. One of those messages, they believed, had been presented to the troops by Sublett, a fellow East Texan.[21] Conflicting views could reflect honest differences about tactics, while individual ambitions could be hard to restrain in a period of apparent success and opportunity. Yet the combination could weaken the resolve and cohesiveness necessary for a successful army—especially one with a democratic system of command.

With his last hope for a major victory lost, Austin announced to the army on November 24 what he had known since the eighteenth; he had been selected by the provisional government to represent the Texan cause in the United States. In the election called by Austin to select a new commander, Edward

Burleson won without serious opposition. By a second vote, 405 enlisted men made a commitment to continue the campaign. These decisions led to a restructuring of the entire organizational system. Only five companies carried over from late November into early December. When the moment came for Austin to proceed to San Felipe, his nephew, Moses Austin Bryan, watched as "the men came up and shook hands with him in tears and silence."[22]

Austin's departure marked an important moment of transition for the Texan army. A new commander would lead a group of mostly new soldiers who had not fought at Gonzales or Concepción. Burleson at forty-two seemed to epitomize the Anglo Texan frontiersman: his family had migrated from North Carolina to Tennessee and then on into Alabama as he grew to maturity. In his teens he had fought against the southern Indians. Soon after his marriage, he migrated to Missouri, where he served in the militia and rose to the rank of colonel. He brought his family to Tennessee in the 1820s and again commanded a militia regiment. After immigrating to Texas during 1829, he settled near Bastrop and served in the Convention of 1833, which petitioned for political reforms. Despite his rapid advance from lieutenant colonel to colonel and then commander in chief of the Texan army in less than two months, Burleson remained an unassuming and casually dressed leader.[23]

The major body of United States volunteers had come in two companies called the New Orleans Greys, which numbered 118 men. They brought more diverse backgrounds to the army, for only 15 of these soldiers had been born in Louisiana, although 42 came from southern states. Twenty-nine had been born in the North, while 26 had immigrated from Europe or Canada, including 10 from England and 9 from Ireland. For the most part, these youthful soldiers were also single and in search of adventure or new opportunities. Some had fought against the Indians of Florida. Both units had been recruited in New Orleans during early October. One company sailed to the Texas coast and landed at Velasco on October 22. After electing leaders there on the Gulf coast, a steamer carried the men to Bra-

37

zoria on the Brazos River. Following food and toasts, they advanced to Victoria and Goliad, gathering untamed mustangs to ride. Some suffered rough spills trying to break the horses, while rain and river fords soaked most of the men at other points. Yet Captain Robert C. Morris led them on to Béxar. The second company traveled by riverboat to Natchitoches, Louisiana; then Captain Thomas H. Breece led his men to San Augustine and Nacogdoches, where they received festive receptions. From there they acquired horses and rode through Washington and Bastrop, reaching San Antonio shortly after Morris and his command. A smaller company from Mississippi also joined the Texan army in late November. These men and the East Texans who arrived after the fight at Concepción balanced their limited military experience with greater enthusiasm for the combat they had not as yet seen.[24]

When Austin called off his final assault plan, the new troops settled into the sprawling camp north of town. Their fresh enthusiasm led them in search of action, and Herman Ehrenberg and others braved Mexican cannon blasts to cross open ground to join Texas artillerymen at the advanced battery position. There they joined in a contest to see who could aim the most accurate cannon shot at the Alamo. A meticulous Deaf Smith, undistracted by Texan yells and Mexican shots, won when his cannonball struck exactly between two windows. Daniel Shipman and his friends amused themselves by chasing cannonballs fired from the Alamo so that the Texan artillery could reuse them. Another day the volunteers exchanged fire with Mexican snipers across the river and drove them back into town. Some of the New Orleans Greys advanced to the small houses at the edge of the settlement, and a Mexican counterattack almost encircled them before Texans rushed to their rescue. From their foray the volunteers could claim as prizes only a few dishes.[25]

While the Texan army received reinforcements, the Mexican commanders sought fresh troops to bolster their defense of Béxar. Ugartechea and his men avoided the Texan cavalry sent to engage them and reached Laredo by November 22. There they met Lieutenant Colonel José Juan Sánchez Navarro with 454 new conscripts. Sánchez Navarro, a veteran of the Mexican war for independence, served as adjutant inspector of Nuevo León and Tamaulipas in the early 1830s. He had guided the untrained and unarmed reinforcements from Saltillo aided by only a few experienced troops. Some escort soldiers had departed while Sánchez Navarro had struggled to get funds for food and clothing. Yet despite delays for a flooded river and freezing winds, he had brought the conscripts to Laredo in stages from September to November. Ugartechea gathered 173 experienced troops from several small units to join the new recruits and on November 26 led his motley column north out of Laredo toward San Antonio.[26]

Burleson kept his troops on alert for the return of Ugartechea or other Mexican movements and communications. Deaf Smith galloped up to the commander north of town at 10:00 A.M. on November 26 to report a Mexican cavalry column southwest from San Antonio roughly five miles. Rumors raised hopes that the troops brought money for Cos' soldiers. Burleson quickly sent Bowie with forty mounted men to skirmish with the Mexican troops and slow their progress. Colonel William H. Jack led 100 men on foot to support the cavalry. Bowie attacked as the fifty Mexican soldiers passed through a ravine only one mile from Béxar. Following an exchange of shots, both sides dismounted and found cover along streambeds. The Texan cavalry drove off a counterattack by the Mexican force. Jack and his infantry heard the firing as they approached Alazan Creek. Sloshing through water up to their waists, the infantry hurried forward. Cos advanced at least fifty of his own foot soldiers and one cannon to cover the return of his horsemen. Because the shooting had stopped, the advancing Texan infantry could not easily determine the Mexican positions and suddenly found themselves in a crossfire between the Mexican cavalry to the right and infantry on the left. In the midst of disorder, the men hugged the ground, except for Colonel Thomas J. Rusk, who led fifteen men to drive off the nearest cavalrymen.

Texan cavalry led by James Swisher joined the infantry in a

ragged advance on the Mexican troops. Edward Burleson's father, James Burleson, galloped forward toward the blazing Mexican muskets with a shout, "Boys, we have but once to die, they are here in the ditch. Charge them." Mexican infantry responded by firing cannister from their cannon three times as they fell back. Mexican cavalry launched three countercharges to seize a rise for a new artillery position. When Texan firepower forced back the mounted men, the infantry of the Morelos Battalion took up the attack. "These men advanced with great coolness and bravery under a destructive fire from our men, preserving . . . strict order and exhibiting no confusion," observed Rusk. The Texans facing this attack had fired and then prepared to use their rifles as clubs to resist bayonets. Texan reinforcements under Swisher suddenly threatened the Mexican cannon, forcing the recall of the Morelos infantry. Cos then withdrew his men into the San Antonio defenses. An opportunity to draw Mexican troops into the open against at least partially protected riflemen again had proved successful for the Texans. Casualties on the Texan side numbered four with wounds and one who disappeared and was next seen in Gonzales. Mexican casualties included at least three killed and fourteen wounded—a majority from the cavalry companies. The Texans found they had captured about forty horses and mules that were loaded with fodder gathered to feed the animals of the Mexican army. Victory in the Grass Fight lifted Texan morale.[27] Yet Burleson and his men knew that they had not driven off the expected Mexican reinforcements or broken Cos' hold on Béxar as November came to a close and winter seemed already upon them.

FIVE

ATTACK AND DEFENSE

Texan pride over victory in the Grass Fight soon paled in the face of approaching winter and unresolved questions about strategy. The East Texans who had arrived at the beginning of November expressed bitter feelings toward some West Texans who had gone home at the end of October and had not returned. Appeals for "Bread Stuff, Coffee & Sugar some salt and Winter-Clothing" reflected the needs of most soldiers. Conflicts over leadership decisions contributed to further unrest. Rather than continue the siege which had not produced success, the United States volunteers considered the alternative of an advance against Matamoros. The departure of such a force would reduce the army of about seven hundred troops at San Antonio by over a hundred men. Captain Robert Coleman "wrote home quite discouraged as to the prospect for battle." After the Grass Fight, Bowie left the army, under orders originally from Austin, to inspect the Texan position at Goliad. If the army withdrew from Béxar, Bowie would have a winter camp ready for defense at the village farther east. He scouted along the San Antonio River with a few men, searching for Mexican horses while traveling to his new post. In early December, Rusk also departed to supervise the gathering of both men and supplies in East Texas.[1]

Several Anglo Texans in Béxar finally convinced Cos to let them depart for Louisiana. John W. Smith, Samuel Maverick, and others traveled south out of San Antonio on December 1 to the Navarro ranch. From there they circled the town to arrive at the Texan position the next day. When they presented their knowledge of the Mexican defenses to Burleson, he called in his officers to consider an attack. Smith, an engineer, could provide special insight into possible weaknesses. Despite some opposition, Burleson ordered an assault at dawn on December 4 in three columns totaling seven hundred men led by Major Robert Morris, Colonel Alexander Somervell, and Colonel William Jack.

As the troops formed at midnight, a shadowy figure seemed to scout the Texan lines and approach the Alamo to speak with a Mexican soldier. A Texas guard reported the incident to Morris. He hurried the information to Burleson, who feared that Cos would be prepared. All of the division commanders also expressed reluctance to advance. Some thought the figure might be Hendrick Arnold, a guide assigned to one attack column who could not be found. Like Austin on earlier occasions, Burleson called off the attack with a sinking sense of frustration.[2]

The order stunned the Texan troops: one believed the shadowy figure had been cows grazing nearby; some damned their leaders openly; and others gathered their equipment and left camp in small groups. Dozens departed. Burleson formed the soldiers who stayed until the morning of the fourth and explained his decision to halt the assault. He then offered to give up command, followed by most of the other officers. Yet he urged an orderly withdrawal with the Texan artillery to Goliad. A sense of confusion and disillusionment dominated the men as they collected their gear and prepared to turn their backs on San Antonio after a siege of six weeks.

As some troops formed to begin the march late in the afternoon, Arnold reappeared. Possibly he had been the unknown figure, seeking information for the Texans or seeing his wife in Béxar. At the same time, a Mexican cavalry officer galloped out of San Antonio to surrender. Jesús Cuellar had become known as "Comanche" because of a period when the Indians held him prisoner. When Texan officers brought him to Burleson, Cuellar described the poor morale among the remaining 570

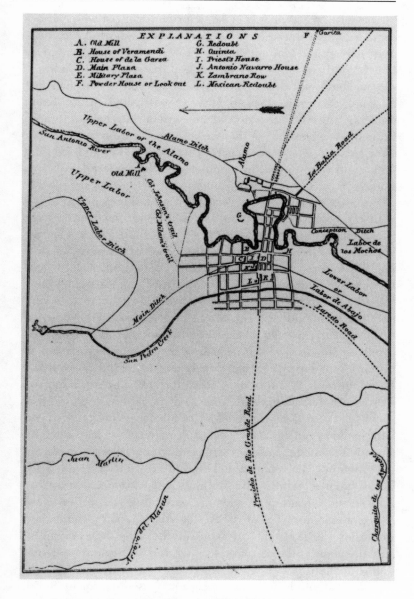

3. *San Antonio in 1835. From Henderson Yoakum,* History of Texas
(New York: Redfield, 1855), II, following p. 26.

Mexican troops. William Cooke, a former druggist who had become a captain in the New Orleans Greys, exhorted the three units of over 100 United States volunteers, who quickly agreed to fight. Others, however, still argued that an attack would result in death and defeat. Ben Milam, an officer who had just rejoined the army, stepped forward and called to the Texan settlers: "Who will go with old Ben Milam into San Antonio?" Probably 200 committed themselves, which brought the attack force to over 300. Others agreed to form reserve and scouting units, and thus the entire command still numbered over 500 soldiers.[3]

Burleson agreed to supervise the operation from a position with the reserves. The men who rallied to make the assault chose Milam to plan and direct the advance into Béxar. A native of Kentucky, Ben Milam had acquired military experience during the War of 1812. He then moved to Louisiana, where he entered trading activities with Spanish colonies, including Mexico. After serving in the James Long foray of 1819 to support the independence movement in Mexico, Milam returned two years later only to be captured for a short time. He served briefly in the army of the new Republic of Mexico, but turned primarily to empresario efforts in Texas with Arthur Wavell and David Burnet. In support of those interests, he attended the legislature of Coahuila and Texas in 1835, where he found that some fellow settlers viewed him as a self-serving land speculator. Soldiers of the national government then arrested him along with state leaders for disregarding new laws of the central government. He soon eluded his guards and celebrated his forty-seventh birthday by finding Texan troops just before they seized Goliad in October. After joining Austin he served as a commander of scouts. The sturdy six-footer came back from these duties to the camp outside Béxar in time to help instill the new enthusiasm that converted disillusionment into determination.[4]

Milam adopted the basic concept proposed earlier by Smith and Maverick, who had been in San Antonio. They pointed to some abandoned buildings on the north side of Béxar as possible footholds from which to launch an attack on nearby houses close to the plazas. To distract Mexican guards, Texan artillery would shell the Alamo east of the river while the main advance came west of the stream.

Early in the evening, Creed Taylor, like many of the Texans, felt "joyous as if waiting a festive affair." When the soldiers first gathered around the mill north of town about 3:00 A.M., several believed their numbers had dwindled, with estimates ranging from 210 to 280 men, and the mood became more somber. Milam resolutely formed the troops in two divisions as stragglers continued to arrive. He would lead the first division on the right, with Major Robert Morris as second in command. During the battle 169 men and officers served in the six companies commanded by John Crane, George English, William Landrum, Thomas Llewellyn, William Patton, and John York, with Maverick and Arnold directing their path that morning. Nidland Franks led a small company that would handle the two cannon attached to the division. The second division on the left would be led by Colonel Francis W. Johnson with Colonels James Grant and William T. Austin sharing the second level of command. Over the next five days, 177 men and officers served in the seven companies of Thomas Alley, Thomas H. Breece, William G. Cooke, Peter J. Duncan, H. H. Edwards, J. W. Peacock, and James G. Swisher. An eighth company under Plácido Benavides contained 25 to 40 additional troops. Deaf Smith and John W. Smith directed the progress of this division.[5] At least 371 men joined the attack.

Colonel James C. Neill guided the movement of a cannon to the east bank of the San Antonio River above the Alamo at 3:00 A.M. A company of Texans under John S. Roberts accompanied the artillery to defend against Mexican attack. Neill fired the first blast at 5:00 A.M. The thudding sound of the cannon, followed by the crash of the cannonball against the wall of the old mission, startled Mexican sentries. Bugle notes alerted the garrison, and a drum roll called the defenders to the walls of the Alamo. The Texan bombardment and Mexican counterfire continued until well after sunrise. Neill then led his detachment back across the river to rejoin Burleson. The battle for Béxar finally had begun.[6]

At the sound of the opening artillery fire before dawn, the two attack columns crept through a cornfield north of San Antonio where the men, to move more quietly, left their equipment. Outside the town, scouts killed a few Mexican pickets before they could cry out. As the Texans climbed through a fence, Mexican guards discovered the advance and shot at them. Deaf Smith quickly picked off at least one sentry. Milam led his column to seize the de la Garza home one block north of the Main Plaza, a distance of between fifty and a hundred yards. Mexican troops had their first clear shot at the Texan advance as Johnson and his men, closer to the river, rushed toward the Veramendi home across the road east of the de la Garza house. Mexican artillery and infantry immediately fired down the street on the Texans, who hugged the walls and leaped for cover behind the rock building. Milam ordered his troops to protect the charge of the second division with rifle and cannon fire. When Mexican troops turned some of their guns on the de la Garza home, Johnson and his soldiers entered the Veramendi home to give the Texans their second stone stronghold.[7]

After sunrise Cos determined that the real threat to his defenses came from the Texans in the houses west of the river. Mexican artillery in the Alamo shifted its aim to create a crossfire with the seven cannon on the plazas. The bombardment "seamed to set fire to earth and skie" as it swept the streets and open ground around the buildings in which the Texans found themselves isolated. One shot knocked a Texan cannon from its carriage. The gunners fired the remaining artillery piece at a range of about 120 yards and toppled one of the Mexican cannon. A Texan saw several of his fellow cannoneers fall around him, while "a ball passed through my hat and cut the flesh to the scull bone and my clothes received many shots." Under such fire the Texan artillerymen finally left their cannon silent in the road as they took cover in the houses.[8]

To fight back, the Texans used crowbars to chop openings in

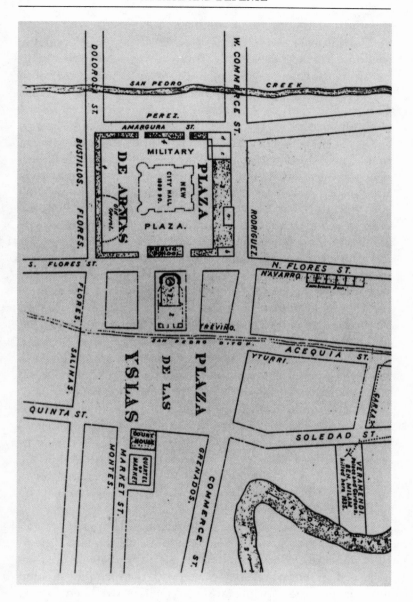

4. San Antonio Plazas. Adapted from William Corner, San Antonio de Bexar *(San Antonio: Bainbridge and Corner, 1890), following p. 16.*

the south walls of the stone buildings. Riflemen began to shoot at Mexican soldiers defending the street barricades and the rooftops. The accuracy of the Texans occasionally drove gunners from the cannon, yet they could never silence the Mexican fusillade which at times found even the gun ports. Ten Texans climbed on top of the Veramendi house to fire from behind the low walls that stood up higher than the flat roof, but Mexican snipers from the tower of the church between the plazas pinned them down with shots from the taller building. A chilling breeze whipped across the Texans, scattering their powder as they tried to load their weapons. Deaf Smith and half of the men fell with wounds. To find shelter the uninjured soldiers used Bowie knives to chop a gap in the roof. Then they let Smith down by a blanket because of his wound.[9]

Despite their strong foothold at the edge of town, the Texans faced serious problems. Mexican fire cut them off from the river or any other source of water. A Mexican Texan woman tried to carry water to the Texans, but a bullet struck her down. To provide water as well as a path of protected movement between the houses, Texans, in the evening, dug trenches and piled the dirt to form earthworks across the road and down to the river. Those in the Veramendi house also reinforced the wall around the yard in the same way. A few men ran the gauntlet of Mexican fire at nightfall to reach the Texan camp for ammunition. When the supply party returned, bringing meat, milk, and bread as well, forty reinforcements joined their sprint across the open area to the stone buildings. Soldiers in the Veramendi house killed a tough ox and a wandering rooster to eat despite Mexican artillery fire which at times dumped the food into the cooking fires.

To silence the most accurate Mexican fire, United States volunteers from the first division assaulted small houses close to them after dark. Under rapid battering the wall of one building collapsed on the occupants. Women with their families shouted for help or in fear, while Mexican soldiers struggled to free themselves from the rubble. The Texans sent them to the rear, the civilians for protection and the soldiers as prisoners. Then the Texans burned what remained of the building. The first day of fighting had cost one dead and fifteen wounded in the Texan attack force.[10]

While the fighting focused on the stone houses, Burleson gathered his reserve force around the mill near the river. When he saw Milam and Johnson successfully capture the buildings, he then withdrew his men to defend their supply base. From there he kept cavalry scouts from the companies of James Cheshire, Robert M. Coleman, John S. Roberts, and Juan Seguín circling the town for any sign of Mexican troops trying to enter or leave. Additional troops who had left earlier returned, along with reinforcements from Goliad. Thus the camp guard came to include the companies of John Bradley, Thomas Borden, Michael Ruth, and Peyton Splann. The presence of over 400 Texan reserves and scouts outside the town forced Cos to retain most of his more than 400 cavalry east of the river to protect the Alamo. Thus the Morelos Battalion, already reduced by losses at Concepción to about 150 men, had to hold the plazas with limited support. At the point of attack, the Texans had an advantage in numbers.[11]

During the second day, Burleson and Milam sent an urgent plea to the Texan government for more troops and artillery ammunition. They added a reminder that Ugartechea might appear at any time to tip the scales against them. When the message reached Governor Henry Smith on December 9, he responded immediately with some munitions as well as a call for new recruits. Moseley Baker reported the situation from the front to the Council with a similar appeal, warning "This army is in danger—Texas is in danger." Yet political divisions continued to plague the army. Governor Smith expressed distrust in Colonel José María Gonzales, who had been sent by the Provisional Council to promote desertions from the units with Cos.[12]

Mexican troops bolstered their defenses around the plazas after dark. When light allowed them to see the Texan positions on the morning of the sixth, Cos ordered his artillery to resume its bombardment. Mexican infantry joined in with muskets. Under the protection of their riflemen, the Texans continued to

49

develop the trench system, which allowed their cannoneers to resume firing. Milam expanded his line by sending Lieutenant William McDonald with men from Crane's unit to capture another building beyond the de la Garza house toward San Pedro Creek. Five Texans suffered wounds on the second day of the struggle, and individual soldiers again dashed across open ground to provide water for the injured men.

Cos sent out troops after dark to construct earthworks east of the river from which his cavalry could support the artillery crossfire from the Alamo. Throughout the morning of December 7, Mexican soldiers renewed and intensified their sniping at the Texan positions. Rifle fire from the Texans proved more accurate, forcing the Mexican troops down behind their walls and barricades by late morning. Well-directed shots from the Texan twelve-pounder cannon also drove Mexicans from the church tower at least briefly. Losses forced Cos to spread his troops thinly and to draft infantry for loading and firing the cannon that defended the plazas. During the lull York's men charged an additional building near the right side of the Texan line. The Mexicans quickly renewed their bombardment. To escape such a precarious position, Henry Karnes used a crowbar to smash down the door. The Texans rushed in, seized the house, and captured several Mexican soldiers.[13]

Milam crossed to the Veramendi home about 3:30 P.M. to confer with Johnson. The Texan leader had identified the Mexican command post between the plazas and the Alamo. To seize Cos and break the deadlock, Milam planned a surprise attack after dark to be led by William Austin. When Milam and Johnson stepped outside to observe the situation from behind the garden walls, a Mexican sharpshooter killed Milam. Although return fire shot the sniper from a tree, Texan morale slumped sharply with the loss of the most experienced and charismatic commander. A sad group of soldiers interred his body in one of the trenches through the yard. The chances of success could slip away without energetic leadership. The specter of Ugartechea with fresh Mexican troops loomed even larger over the embattled assault force. The Texan officers gathered about 7:00

P.M. and selected Colonel Francis W. Johnson to assume direction of the attack.[14]

At the age of thirty-six, Frank Johnson brought a diversity of
experience to his new position of command. He had grown up
in Tennessee, where his family had settled after his birth in Virginia. In the following years, he had ranged about from land
surveying in Alabama to teaching and business endeavors in Il-
linois and mining in Missouri. When he contracted malaria
after freighting goods on the Mississippi River in 1826, he came
to Texas to convalesce. He traveled through several colonies
and surveyed around San Augustine before devoting himself to
the duties of alcalde for San Felipe. When conflict occurred at
Anahuac in 1832, Johnson's intense commitment led to his election as an officer in the Texan force. Later he chaired a committee during the Convention of 1832. Before the attack on Béxar,
he had served Austin and Burleson as adjutant and inspector
general. As a proven leader with some military experience and
a full understanding of the battle plan, Johnson received strong
support.[15]

Robert C. Morris replaced Milam as commander of the
Texan right wing. To boost morale and to further strengthen
their position, he directed the companies of Crane, English,
Landrum, and Llewellyn to attack the Antonio Navarro home,
which was north of the church and even nearer the plazas,
about 10:00 P.M. Drizzle and falling temperature created harsh
conditions, but the weather provided cover and helped the
Texans surprise the defenders and seize the building. In a counterattack Mexican troops climbed on top of the house and tried
to cave in the roof, but rifle fire forced them down. Besides the
crucial shot that killed Milam, two other Texans were shot but
survived on the third day of fighting.[16]

Mexican spirits soared on the morning of December 8, despite a chilling rain, when Ugartechea found his way past Texan
scouting parties with the long-awaited reinforcements. Lieutenant Colonel José Juan Sánchez Navarro had brought 454
newly conscripted men from Saltillo to Laredo during late October and early November. There they had met Ugartechea and

resumed their march toward Béxar on November 26 with an escort of 173 more experienced troops, including artillery, cavalry, and infantry. Sánchez Navarro found that "we were greeted with rifle fire, acclamations and ringing of bells" when they entered San Antonio. To the Texans who were unaware of the cause, martial music from the Mexican band created concern. "It appeared we were to be sweap of[f] by a general charge by the Cavilry infantry and lancers," thought one Texan soldier. Cos added further foreboding to the occasion by flying a black flag over his position to imply that he would give no quarter to his opponents. Yet an inspection of his new troops left Cos with serious concerns: "they lacked training; were tired from a twenty three league march to the city; and they only aggravated matters by increasing the consumption of provisions of which there was an absolute lack."[17]

Despite worries about a possible improvement in the Mexican situation, the Texans refused to stand on the defensive. Johnson reinforced the troops in the Navarro home with some of the United States volunteers. To capture the neighboring buildings known as Zambrano Row, the Texans advanced around 9:00 A.M. Rushing across the open space between buildings to avoid Mexican fire, they hacked their way through bolted windows and doors using crowbars and axes. With the same tools, they began to tunnel through the heavy stone walls, one room at a time, to avoid the musket and cannon fire outside. Mexican soldiers fought to defend each room. Men fired on each other through holes in the walls at short range. The combatants took on a ghostly appearance as crumbling mortar covered them. During lulls in the fighting, the troops debated, taunted, and dared each other from opposite sides of a wall. By late afternoon the Texans held the entire building. They stopped then to enjoy some captured cornbread and to distribute powder left behind by the Mexican troops. Three Texans had received wounds in the struggle.[18]

With the addition of some new men—the escort troops—who could join the fighting immediately, Cos sought to counterattack by seizing the Texan supply base with a sudden thrust along the river. From there he hoped to strike at the rear of the Texan assault force, which might be encircled and captured. Part of the Mexican cavalry rode out of the Alamo, led by Captains Don Manuel Barragán and Don Manuel Lafuente, and moved north along the east bank of the river late in the day. Burleson met the mounted force by moving two companies to face them, under cover of artillery fire. The Mexican troops shot at the Texans from long range, but never delivered the charge Cos originally had planned.[19]

In the evening about seven o'clock, Johnson sent the four companies of Alley, Duncan, Edwards, and Swisher from his left wing to strengthen the Texan hold on Zambrano Row. Burleson ordered forward one hundred fresh troops in the three companies under James Cheshire, M. B. Lewis, and William Sutherland to help hold the other houses.[20]

As those movements took place, around 9:00 P.M., Cos ordered heavy cannon and musket fire near the west bank of the river. Ehrenberg found "our walls were shattered, almost leveled to the ground, and the best we could do was to seek refuge behind the crumbling stones or falling adobe." When the Mexican troops did not attempt a charge, however, some Texans sallied out to disrupt the nearest Mexican positions.[21]

With his second division holding its buildings and with men in position for a further advance on the right by 10:30 P.M., Johnson ordered William Cooke to lead about fifty men of the New Orleans Greys and Patton's Brazoria unit in a night assault to establish a foothold on the plazas. Moonlight exposed their movements to a renewed Mexican crossfire. J. W. Smith guided them to the Yturri home, only to face a door too strong to be quickly broken down. To escape the precarious position, Cooke led the troops in a crawl along the house wall so close to the gun slits that the Mexican troops could not aim down at the sharp angle necessary to hit the attackers. The Texans then leaped a wall to reach the plaza, where they immediately came under a new fusillade from Mexican soldiers. Pressed to get his men under cover, Cooke found an entrance with an open archway above it, which allowed his men to shoot into the home of Fa-

ther Refugio de la Garza and force out its defenders, who were
tired after four days of combat with little rest. The Texans captured several women, boys, and girls and sent them to rooms
away from the fighting.

To silence a Mexican cannon only a few yards from the house,
Cooke led his men back into the plaza. Mexican troops under
Condelle and Sánchez Navarro responded to bugle calls and
rallied. Their fire, along with the artillery, forced the Texans
back into the building and wounded John Belden as he raced
for cover after trying to disable the cannon. From Father de la
Garza they heard for the first time that Ugartechea had returned with more soldiers. Suddenly their advanced position
appeared "hopeless." A gap had opened between the Texan divisions as their line spread to include more buildings. Captain
York lost touch with Cooke and reported the assault group
probably had been slain. When Burleson learned of the fresh
Mexican soldiers, he immediately appealed to the Texan government for more troops and supplies. "Send us help and we
never will quit the field untill we can Enjoy our Constitutional
rites." He communicated his concern to Johnson and suggested
a withdrawal from the town. Retreat seemed a real considera-
tion. The night appeared much darker.[22]

Cooke and his men worked feverishly to strengthen their
position in the priest's house. They used Bowie knives to loosen
the earth underfoot and pile it against the walls. To block every
opening, the Texans heaped up chests and other furniture. Yet
the Mexican artillery blew holes in these defenses. "Several
Balls came through and fell in the floor" among the Texans.
"[Determ]ined to sell our lives as dearly as possible," Cooke
gave his men a choice: "retreat, Surrender, or die." His tired
soldiers agreed to hang on, although short of powder.[23]

Across the plaza the Mexicans found their position equally
critical. Condelle placed Sánchez Navarro in charge of two cannon protected by burial headstones and facing the Texans in the
home on the north side of the square. To aid the twenty soldiers
that Sánchez Navarro originally had gathered, Cos sent him ten
regular infantry as well as eighty of the newly arrived con-

scripts. Having escorted them to Béxar, Sánchez Navarro knew that they "did not know even how to load," however, and "did nothing more than add to the confusion." At his request Condelle pulled them out of the line and brought up cavalrymen to stabilize the position.[24]

Since the Texans could sweep the plaza with rifle fire when daylight came, Cos decided to consolidate his defensive position by withdrawing from the town to the mission. About one o'clock Mexican mounted companies began to pull back. Sánchez Navarro with the two cannon and about fifty men of the Morelos and Tamaulipas units acted as a rear guard at the plaza. The sounds of battle dwindled around three o'clock, followed by occasional shots.

In the Alamo, Mexican cavalry officers rejected orders for a counterattack. The sounds of battle echoing through the town had convinced them that the Texans might surround their entire position. Morale among the cavalrymen probably had been disrupted further by a published appeal from José María Gonzales, the federalist colonel who had joined the Texans in November. He urged his "countrymen" and fellow soldiers to oppose centralism "and restore liberty to your country." Four officers gathered soldiers from at least four of the cavalry companies, led them out of the mission fortress, and rode south. Individuals from other units joined them. When Cos rushed through the blackness, shouting to stop the defection, the men did not recognize or understand him. As the horses galloped past, they jostled the general, and the thudding hooves almost ran him down. Remaining soldiers who witnessed the hurried departure and the shadowy buffeting of their commander thought he had been killed and wondered aloud: "What shall we do?" The startling exit of the horsemen created chaos and frightened the military wives, sons, and daughters who had been sent to the Alamo for safety, and some rushed into the night calling out questions. Word of the situation spread to the troops on the plaza and created concern but no collapse.

With about 120 experienced infantry left as fighting resumed at six o'clock, Cos called Sánchez Navarro to the Alamo. Reluctantly the general directed his tired subordinate to "go save those brave men. I authorize you to approach the enemy and obtain the best terms possible." When Sánchez Navarro returned to the plaza, he met Condelle, who was directing a slow retreat to better cover. Yet the colonel argued against negotiations, for "the Morelos Battalion has never surrendered." Other officers joined the dispute, but Sánchez Navarro reminded them that he had fought until ordered to approach the Texans. With two other officers, he continued on his mission.[25]

When bugle calls brought no response from the Texans, Sánchez Navarro raised a truce flag at the plaza about seven o'clock on December 9. With a sense of relief, William Cooke advanced out of the priest's home to meet him and to lead the Mexican officers to Colonel Johnson. Father de la Garza entered the group which then sent for Burleson. Uneasily the Mexican officers waited two hours amid the Texan troops until Burleson arrived. He threatened to hold the officers as prisoners because they had no written instructions from Cos. When a Mexican officer brought back the necessary explanation, Burleson appointed Johnson, Morris, and James Swisher to negotiate. Working through the afternoon with Miguel Arciniega and John Cameron as interpreters, the Texans rejected early Mexican requests that they be allowed to retire with their weapons and equipment. After continued talks in the evening, the representatives of both armies finally settled on an eighteen-point agreement at two o'clock the next morning.[26]

Under the terms of the treaty, the Mexican officers received paroles which required them to leave by the sixth day, to withdraw "into the interior," and no longer to resist the Constitution of 1824. With them would go the remaining Mexican troops, including the new replacements, with ten bullets each and one small cannon for protection from Indian attack. Those who had broken away from Cos could stay or leave with him or depart separately. All other weapons and supplies would be surrendered to the Texans after an inventory by three officers from each army. To avoid conflict the Mexican troops would remain in the mission, while the Texans would stay in San Antonio until Cos departed, although both groups could cross the river unarmed. Mexican wounded could be left with a doctor in San Antonio if they could not travel. Prisoners taken in the fighting would be freed. The Texans would sell supplies to the Mexicans for the march to Laredo. Private citizens could safely reclaim any property lost during the battle.[27]

While the officers negotiated, the soldiers wandered through the town. To Henry Dance "every thing looked miserable . . . heaps of dirt and Stone ashes from the burning of Some wood breast works . . . with dead animals lieing about cannon balls & shot of every discription thick on the ground with the plastering shot of[f] the outside of the walls of the houses." He and his friends enjoyed a meal of tortillas with honey, meat, corn, and liquor which preceded their first good night of sleep in a week.[28]

About 10:00 A.M. on December 11, Johnson paraded the volunteer army for its last democratic act. To the Texan troops, he presented the terms of surrender and argued for their approval because the army had little ammunition left with which to continue fighting. When the companies voted, most men accepted the treaty with relief, although a minority favored harsher terms and later called the agreement "a child's bargain." By afternoon some soldiers from the opposing armies began to mingle and even entered into peaceful competition over cards. The victors celebrated the official end of hostilities with a lively fandango that evening.[29]

The 30 to 35 Texas casualties, including 5 or 6 killed in the assault, could not join the celebration by the rest of the 780 men who participated in the battle, guarded the camp, and scouted. Old settlers and new volunteers from the United States shared Texan losses about equally. Among them lay Greenberry Logan, a free black man who had served since October.

Mexican casualties remained partially unreported. Eight of the twelve cavalry companies reported only 3 killed and 6 wounded for December 5–9, 1835. The remaining mounted units probably met with similarly light losses. Yet the infantry who defended the plazas suffered much heavier losses, prob-

ably about 100 killed, wounded, and missing. Since infantry replaced injured artillerymen, that small group must have suffered heavy losses like the foot soldiers. Thus it seems probable
that about 150 of the men with Cos died, suffered wounds, or
were captured during the five days of fighting. Texan physicians
helped treat the serious wounds of several Mexican soldiers
who could not leave when Cos marched south on the fourteenth. With him went about 800 men, including the new recruits brought by Ugartechea, but not the cavalrymen who had
left on the ninth. Before he departed the Mexican general delivered to the Texans over 400 small arms, twenty cannon, and
assorted supplies, uniforms, and equipment.

Johnson assumed leadership of the remaining troops in the
volunteer army on December 15, when Burleson and many of
the veterans left San Antonio to rejoin their families. As the
men rode out of Béxar that day, the Texas General Council met
in San Felipe to hear the exciting news of their "glorious victory." While expressing sadness at the death of Milam, the
delegates proclaimed the soldiers to be "the brave sons of
Washington and freedom."[30]

After the surrender some additional Texan and United States
volunteers arrived with a heavy artillery piece, the type the
Texans had waited for in vain over a span of several weeks. The
men who had labored to bring the cannon such a distance con-
soled themselves with the belief that Cos had abandoned hope
of further defense when he learned of their advance.[31]

The longer range of the Texans' rifles had not provided as
much advantage in the house-to-house fighting as it had during
earlier confrontations in the field. Yet the greater accuracy of
the Texans' rifles had allowed them a continued dominance in
firepower. Still, victory could not be assumed in such situa-
tions. Texans would fight house-to-house battles again in Mexico in 1842 at Mier, where they surrendered, and in 1846 at
Monterrey, where they prevailed.[32]

Mexican supply and morale problems at San Antonio had
become greater in the final days of combat. The Texans had

achieved success at Béxar because of two factors. New information about Mexican defenses and conditions had turned pessimism to optimism and a retreat into an advance on December 4 and 5. Then, on December 9, when each army found itself in a critical situation, without a clear sense of enemy conditions, the Texans persevered, perhaps because they had greater control of the area surrounding the town. To their surprise they accepted the surrender of the disrupted Mexican army, which knew it had no hope of immediate supplies across the arid region between San Antonio and Laredo.

SIX

CONCLUSIONS

The campaign and victory at San Antonio shaped the future course of the Texas Revolution. Bowie, Travis, and Fannin established themselves as successful junior officers in cavalry raids, the battle of Concepción, and in the Grass Fight. As a result, they would rise to command at the Alamo and at Goliad in early 1836. Yet each had exhibited intense ambition or a touchy sense of honor, or both, in the Béxar campaign. Fannin and Travis had left the volunteer army before the final assault on San Antonio, while Bowie had been assigned other duties at the time. These traits produced strong but sometimes uncooperative leaders. Each of them became a martyr to the Texas cause and attained varying degrees of heroic stature. Yet none achieved military victory as completely independent commanders. At least seventy-nine veterans of the fighting at San Antonio, mostly recent volunteers from the United States, died with these leaders, fifty or more in the Álamo and at least twenty-nine at Goliad.

One of the men captured with Fannin in the spring of 1836 concluded, "His former experience in fighting Mexicans had led him to entertain a great contempt for them as soldiers, and led him to neglect to take such precautionary measures as were requisite." Had Fannin stayed through the attack on Béxar, he might have gained a more realistic assessment of his adversaries. Yet the fighting at Concepción should have taught him lessons on Mexican courage and the value of a good defensive position. His status as joint commander with Bowie on that occasion may have hidden his own limitations as a leader.[1]

Travis added to his reputation for aggressive action by capturing a Mexican horse herd. Yet that success provided little experience for the complications of shared command in a defensive position such as the Alamo.

Bowie had shown defensive ability at Concepción, then had moved rapidly to engage the Mexican cavalry at the Grass Fight. Thus he exhibited diverse talents and achieved more success than most Texas officers during the campaign. His claim to a position of command in the future seemed one of the strongest among the revolutionary leaders.

Sam Houston, the man who was not there, provided the most intriguing figure among the Texans. Although he visited the volunteer army briefly at Salado Creek in late October, Houston never came within sight of San Antonio. Austin's staff and others believed that Houston sought command, however, and that he suffered considerable depression and frustration when the troops did not turn to him for leadership. Then and on other occasions, he expressed doubts about the potential success of the campaign and sought to divert men and supplies to the regular army of which he later became general. His friends seem to have led the opposition to several proposals of attack by Stephen F. Austin and Edward Burleson. Houston's cautious advice reflected military experience and foreshadowed his strategy through much of the San Jacinto campaign. From that battle to the Civil War, Houston showed considerable insights and achieved major successes in war and politics. Yet in 1835 he remained a relatively new settler who like many others hoped to advance his fortunes in a time of flux and opportunity.

Stephen F. Austin deserves recognition for uniting and maintaining the Texan volunteer army over a span of six weeks despite problems with discipline and supplies as well as his own poor health. Although Austin had only limited military experience, like Abraham Lincoln a generation later, the Texan leader quickly came to understand the need to defeat the opposing army. He also saw the value of eliminating any stronghold in

Texas that could serve as a base for Mexican forces. Political duties ultimately called Austin away before the final victory, yet he did more than anyone to prepare for that moment of success.

Edward Burleson provided a sense of continuity and commitment as the only ranking officer to serve throughout the San Antonio campaign. He shared Austin's desire to defeat the Mexican army. Thus when his own plan of attack met opposition, he stayed to support the volunteer assault force that emerged. The presence of Burleson with his camp guards and scouting companies forced Martín Perfecto de Cos to retain troops in the Alamo, an action that weakened defense of the plazas.

Ben Milam became the charismatic figure who crystallized support for an attack at the crucial moment. The assault under his leadership established the foothold from which success might be achieved. His death during the battle created a momentary morale problem but provided the Texans with their first martyr to the revolutionary cause.

Frank Johnson rallied the volunteers from their mourning for Milam to complete the storming of San Antonio. He survived an unsuccessful expedition toward Matamoros in the spring of 1836 and in later years led the Texas Veterans Association.

William G. Cooke assisted Milam in gathering volunteers for the assault. He then led the crucial capture of the priest's home which gave the Texans a foothold on the plazas and brought on Mexican surrender.

Juan Seguín brought a considerable number of Mexican Texans to the Texan cause, which converted San Antonio into a less hospitable post for Cos. José María Gonzales further undermined morale among the Mexican troops with his federalist appeal to them.

Texan troops elected most of these leaders and voted on battle plans in a striking show of democracy. Yet the decisions also reflected conflicting ambitions as well as differing strategies. Democracy could on occasion become poor discipline and short-term commitments—the failings of volunteer soldiers. Yet in three battles and lesser skirmishes, they fought with ability and enthusiasm. Ultimately they achieved the victory they had sought for two months. The greater range and accuracy of their rifles provided a firepower advantage that proved significant in each clash. The unplanned turnover of troops, with East Texans and United States volunteers replacing many of the original soldiers from the Brazos and Colorado valleys, kept the Texan army fresh and helped wear down its opponents.

The United States volunteers provided new enthusiasm that helped sustain the army in the final days of the siege. Yet their presence contributed to the Mexican view that Texan opposition stemmed from outside influences. That belief may have contributed in turn to Santa Anna's order of "no quarter" in his 1836 campaign.[2] As the number of United States volunteers grew in the following weeks, the Texan forces became less representative of the state than the army that had captured San Antonio.

When most of the Texan volunteers dispersed after taking Béxar, they left only a small garrison in the town. Thus San Antonio immediately became vulnerable to the return of a new Mexican army during the succeeding days. Success of the democratic Texan army in the fall of 1835 probably delayed the acceptance of a coordinated command system and thus contributed to defeats in the spring of 1836.

At the head of the opposing army, Martín Perfecto de Cos conducted a careful defense of Béxar. Especially after the unsuccessful foray at Concepción, he strengthened the fortifications and sought to conserve both his men and limited supplies. Domingo de Ugartechea and José Juan Sánchez Navarro made an impressive forced march to bring replacements, although a lack of time for training left those conscripts unable to contribute much to the defense. Nicolás Condelle, commander of the Morelos Battalion, led a tenacious defense, arguing against surrender even when there seemed little choice.

The Mexican troops, especially the infantry of the Morelos Battalion, showed courage in their repeated attacks at Concepción and again in the Grass Fight. Stubbornly they fought to hold the plazas against the final assault. Dwindling supplies, the frustration of being restricted to the town for two months, and an undercurrent of federalist sentiment created nagging morale problems and wore down the Mexican troops. A trickle of desertions suddenly became a burst of confusion during the final night of combat. When several cavalry units withdrew, Cos was forced to negotiate. Sánchez Navarro sensed the long-range significance of the moment: "All has been lost save honor!"[3]

Caught between the two armies, the Mexican Texans of San Antonio suffered internal divisions and military suspicions as men served on both sides. To avoid the fighting, many civilians left town for the nearby ranches, only to return in some cases to battered or burned homes. The nearby ranch owners lost cattle and crops to each army in return for sporadic and incomplete promises of payment. Thus the civilians, too, faced shortages.

When Cos returned as part of the Mexican army in the spring of 1836, Texans believed he had broken his parole in the surrender agreement. Yet if Cos were to remain an officer, he had little choice, for he recrossed the Rio Grande under orders from Santa Anna. By the time Cos fought at the Alamo, Texas political leaders had declared for independence and had passed beyond the Constitution of 1824, which Cos had promised not to oppose. The conflict had evolved past the level of December 1835. Cos survived capture at San Jacinto and appeared again during 1847 as a military officer in the war between the United States and Mexico. Sánchez Navarro, who also fought at the Alamo, served on the Indian frontier in northern Mexico and became a general after the conflict with the United States.

Despite their own conflicting personalities and strategies, the Texans gained control of San Antonio and forced the Mexican army entirely out of Texas. In doing so they shaped Santa Anna's plans for 1836. "Bexar was held by the enemy," in his eyes, "and it was necessary to open the door to our future operations by taking it." Ignoring advice from subordinates to bypass the town, the Mexican commander in chief focused his counterthrust at San Antonio in early 1836.[4] The failure of Cos to hold the town plazas probably influenced Texan commanders to concentrate their troops in the Alamo during the spring of 1836. The efforts by Cos to strengthen the Alamo walls and to construct several earthen mounds as cannon mounts inside, along with the artillery surrendered by the Mexican army, contributed to the later Texan defense of the old mission. The cannon that helped delay Santa Anna's advance also helped set the stage for the Texan victory at San Jacinto.[5]

Over ninety veterans from the battle for Béxar, perhaps a hundred, led by Edward Burleson, joined in achieving the final Texan triumph at San Jacinto.[6] Several went on to lead the new Republic of Texas. Burleson became its vice-president in the 1840s. Thomas William Ward, who lost a leg in the attack on San Antonio, served two terms as commissioner of the General Land Office. William G. Cooke acted as secretary of war and marine for the new nation. Ward and Cooke, although former comrades in arms, clashed after the revolution and almost fought duels on two occasions. Among those who preceded Cooke as secretary of war, Thomas J. Rusk went on to become a United States senator after the annexation of Texas. Twenty-two counties in the state came to carry the names of men who had fought at Béxar.[7]

A grateful Texan government provided bounty land grants of 320 acres and donation grants of 640 acres to those who could prove that they had participated in the capture of San Antonio. Officials certified 504 veterans for a bounty or a donation grant or both, including 63 Mexican Texans and 2 free blacks. For later service in the spring campaigns of 1836, 121 additional veterans of Béxar or their heirs received bounty or donation grants. At least 7, possibly 10, of these men built upon their land grants to join an elite group of 263 Texans worth $100,000 or more in 1860. Three of the veterans, Edward Burleson, Ezekiel W. Cullen, and Samuel Maverick founded families that continued to provide political or civic leadership in Texas well into the twentieth century.[8]

Regardless of their economic status, the veterans remembered the siege of San Antonio and understood its significance as the initial victory that paved the way for the later military and political success of the Texan revolt. Many of them would have agreed with Thomas Lubbock that "the storming of Bexar" had been "the most glorious feat of arms of the Texas revolution."[9] Richard Santos captured the importance of the battle: "The departure of the forces under Cos was the turning point in the struggle for Texas independence. Hereafter, all Mexican troops in Texas would be invaders, not defenders, and Texas was destined to remain Texan evermore."[10]

THE TEXAN AND MEXICAN ARMIES AT BÉXAR

TEXAN ARMY

The number of men in the Texan army at San Antonio varied constantly from October into December because of its democratic organization. Stephen F. Austin estimated 300 soldiers at Gonzales on October 12, when he advanced on Béxar. By the nineteenth he reported a strength of 450. At the end of October, the number had grown to 600 men. After a brief decline in army strength as a result of colder weather, new reinforcements brought the command to a peak of 800 soldiers by November 7. With some fluctuations the army remained at about 700 to 800 men through the rest of the month.

Despite the traditional figure of 300 men in the Texan assault force at Béxar on December 5, and some estimates of only 210 to 280 in the initial attack, a larger number of Texans ultimately fought at San Antonio. The muster rolls of the two divisions which initially entered the town contain 346 names. To these should be added the two artillery companies—15 men under Nidland Franks, according to Frank Johnson, and 18 on the muster roll of T. L. F. Parrott's company, which probably served the cannon for James Neill. Plácido Benavides' company, which served with the second division, numbered 25 to 40 soldiers, whose omission is noted on the muster rolls. Edward Burleson later sent into the battle the companies of James Cheshire, William Sutherland, and M. B. Lewis. The muster roll for

Cheshire's men shows 35, while the roll of Lewis' company listed 34 men. William Austin estimated that the three companies totaled 100 men. John Roberts' company of about 20 men protected Neill's artillery, while John M. Bradley's company of 37 men met the Mexican cavalry foray against Burleson's camp. Thus approximately 561 Texans engaged in the fighting at Béxar in December. In addition, the companies of Peyton Splann, Michael Ruth, and Thomas W. Borden protected army supplies in camp, while the company of Robert M. Coleman helped scout for Mexican reinforcements. Since companies composed of Texan settlers averaged 21 men, these four units probably contained at least 80 men. Mexican Texan scouting companies under Juan Seguín included about 135 troops. These men brought the entire Texan army to approximately 776 soldiers. Further support for the concept of a larger Texan force comes from the list of 504 men who received land grants for their service at San Antonio. That list in turn does not contain the names of 278 men who appear on muster rolls and in other accounts of the battle. The combined total of those figures is 782.

It seems probable that 200 to 300 of the early Texan recruits left the army between late October and early December. Of the 106 men on two company rolls for October 19–20, 26 fought in the final attack on Béxar while 80 had departed. Thus over 1,000 Texans served during the campaign against San Antonio.

MEXICAN ARMY

The exact size of the Mexican army at San Antonio is not easy to determine. The presidial cavalry companies reported from 364 to 382 men and officers between August 1 and October 1, 1835. Yet no more than half of those soldiers were available for duty at one time. The Morelos Battalion of infantry contained about 200 effective troops by the beginning of October. Martín Perfecto de Cos landed with additional cavalry in September and brought them to Béxar by October 9. Samuel Maverick, a Texan who was under house arrest in San Antonio, observed the Mexican army and spoke with Mexican officers. He estimated the troops ready for duty at 647 on October 18. In late October, Cos received 100 reinforcements. Thus the Mexican army numbered about 750 men at that time. Austin estimated 800 to 900.

In the fighting at Concepción on October 27, casualties in the Mexican army included 53 to 60 killed and wounded, reducing it to about 690 men. Stephen F. Austin estimated 700 Mexican troops in early November. Domingo de Ugartechea took 100 cavalry with him when he left in mid-November, while skirmishes and the Grass Fight inflicted at least 20 casualties in the Mexican ranks. Thus Cos probably had about 570 men at the beginning of December. Miguel A. Sánchez Lamego estimates 600 Mexican troops in November.

During the fighting, December 5–9, 1835, eight Mexican cavalry companies lost 3 killed and 6 wounded. The losses of the infantry and artillery who held the plazas have never been completely reported. Cos spoke of 100 regular infantry remaining as he retreated to Laredo after the battle, which suggests about 100 casualties in that unit. Texan estimates of total Mexican losses ranged from 150 to 740 killed and wounded. Vicente Filisola notes several casualties but is not specific. William Cooke and Creed Taylor mention at least 20 prisoners. Thus a total of 150 losses for the Mexican forces appears to be a reasonable figure. That would have reduced the size of Cos' original forces to 420 men. José Juan Sánchez Navarro estimated 300 defenders when he arrived on the fourth day of fighting.

On December 8, Ugartechea returned with about 625 men, of whom 454 were untrained new recruits. That increased the Mexican army to approximately 1,045 men of whom 590 would have been effective soldiers. Burleson estimated 1,300 Mexican troops, which probably was based upon assumptions about the size of the Mexican army on December 5 and the number of reinforcements. Desertions from Cos' forces on the last day of the battle have been estimated at 190 by Filisola and over 200 by Sánchez Lamego, although Sánchez Navarro reported rumors of up to 400. Burleson placed the number at 195. This would have reduced the Mexican army to approximately 855 men, of whom about 400 would have been effective troops. Cos estimated 120 infantry and some cavalry were still capable of resisting an attack. When Cos departed San Antonio after the surrender, Burleson estimated the Mexican army at 1,105. Cos first claimed only 500 to 600, including the new recruits. He counted 815 men when he reached Laredo, however, but described only 100 infantry as effective troops.

TEXAN ORDER OF BATTLE

November 2, 1835, Stephen F. Austin commanding

Upper Division	Colonel John H. Moore
Companies	Thomas Alley
	Valentine Bennet
	Mathew Caldwell
	Jacob Eberly
	Michael R. Goheen
	Byrd Lockhart
	James G. Swisher
	James C. Neill (artillery)
Lower Division	Colonel James Bowie
Companies	Andrew Briscoe
	Robert M. Coleman
	James W. Fannin, Jr.
	Thomas J. Rusk
	T. L. F. Parrott (artillery)
Scouting	Juan Seguín
Companies	William B. Travis

December 5, 1835, Edward Burleson commanding

First Division Companies	Colonel Benjamin R. Milam John Crane George English William Landrum Thomas Llewellyn William Patton John York Nidland Franks (artillery)
Second Division Companies	Colonel Francis W. Johnson Thomas Alley Plácido Benavides Thomas H. Breece William G. Cooke Peter J. Duncan H. H. Edwards J. W. Peacock James G. Swisher
Reserve and Scouting Companies	Thomas W. Borden John M. Bradley James Cheshire Robert M. Coleman M. B. Lewis John S. Roberts Michael Ruth Juan Seguín Peyton Splann William Sutherland James C. Neill (artillery)

MEXICAN ORDER OF BATTLE

General Martín Perfecto de Cos commanding
Permanent Battalion of Morelos, Colonel Nicholás Condelle
Presidial Cavalry Corps, Colonel Domingo de Ugartechea

Companies   Agua Verde
Álamo, First
Álamo, Second
Bavia
Béxar
Lampazos
Nuevo León, First
Nuevo León, Second
Pueblo
Río Grande
Tamaulipas, First
Tamaulipas, Second

NOTES

1. INTRODUCTION

1. The terms Anglo American, Anglos, and Anglo Texans have been used here to describe those persons whose families had come from the British Isles to the British colonies in North America or to the United States in the years prior to the 1830s. Although there is scholarly discussion of the differences between persons of English and Celtic ancestry, that issue does not seem to be a major influence on the events considered in this volume. Thus more complex and perhaps distracting terminology has not been employed. When significant numbers of recent immigrants from Europe participated in these events their presence is carefully noted.

2. TWO ARMIES

1. Dudley G. Wooten, ed., *A Comprehensive History of Texas, 1685 to 1897*, I, 538–540; Moses Austin Bryan, "Recollections of Stephen F. Austin," 15–16, Moses Austin Bryan Papers, Eugene C. Barker Texas History Center, University of Texas at Austin.

2. Wooten, *A Comprehensive History of Texas*, I, 540, Noah Smithwick, *The Evolution of a State; or, Recollections of Old Texas Days*, 74; John H. Jenkins, ed., *The Papers of the Texas Revolution, 1835–1836*, II, 81–82; Alex. W. Terrell, "Stephen F. Austin: A Memorial Address," *Southwestern Historical Quarterly* 14 (January 1911): 186; Moses Austin Bryan, "Recollections of Stephen F. Austin," 14, Bryan Papers.

3. Jenkins, *Papers of the Texas Revolution*, II, 31–32.

4. Eugene C. Barker, *The Life of Stephen F. Austin: Founder of Texas, 1793–1836*, 21–22, 92–96, 171–174.

5. Jenkins, *Papers of the Texas Revolution*, II, 109; Walter Prescott Webb, H. Bailey Carroll, and Eldon Branda, eds., *The Handbook of Texas*, I, 249, II, 229–230, 636–637.

6. Jenkins, *Papers of the Texas Revolution*, II, 92–93, 108–109; Smithwick, *Evolution of a State*, 71–73; James W. Pohl and Stephen L. Hardin, "The Military History of the Texas Revolution: An Overview," *Southwestern Historical Quarterly* 89 (January 1986): 282, 285–286.

7. Jenkins, *Papers of the Texas Revolution*, I, 487, 507, 509, II, 16, 25, 28; Wooten, *Comprehensive History of Texas*, I, 536–539; Miles S. Bennet, "The Battle of Gonzales, the 'Lexington' of the Texas Revolution," *Southwestern Historical Quarterly* 2 (April 1899): 313–315; Companies at Cibolo, October 17, 1835, Stephen F. Austin Papers, Series IV, Barker Texas History Center, University of Texas at Austin. This profile of the Texan army is based upon the list of soldiers who received land grants for service at Béxar in Thomas Lloyd Miller, *Bounty and Donation Land Grants of Texas, 1835–1888;* Muster Rolls in the Archives of the Texas State Library; and Muster Rolls in the Archives of the Texas General Land Office; most of which have been published in Daughters of the Republic of Texas, *Muster Rolls of the Texas Revolution;* as well as lists in Jenkins, *Papers of the Texas Revolution;* and in D. W. C. Baker, comp., *A Texas Scrap Book.* Information about these soldiers has been drawn from the *Handbook of Texas;* Villamae Williams, ed., *Stephen F. Austin's Register of Families;* Gifford White, *1830 Citizens of Texas;* Gifford White, *Character Certificates in the General Land Office of Texas;* and Lester G. Bugbee, "The Old Three Hundred," *Southwestern Historical Quarterly* 1 (October 1897): 108–117.

8. Information on military service comes from Marie Bennet Urwitz, "Valentine Bennet," *Southwestern Historical Quarterly* 9 (January 1906): 145–146; Boyce House, "An Incident at Velasco," *Southwestern Historical Quarterly* 64 (July 1960): 92–95; Jenkins, *Papers of the Texas Revolution*, I, 141–142, 154, 157–158, 161, 178–182, 185–186, 225, 251–252, 311, 455–457, 467, 477–479, 484–485; Nugent E. Brown, *The Book of Nacogdoches County*, 23–31; Frank Lawrence Owsley, Jr., *Struggle for the Gulf Borderlands: The Creek War and the Battle of New Orleans, 1812–1815*, 31–82, 144–166.

9. Jenkins, *Papers of the Texas Revolution*, II, 102–103, 108–109, 118–119, 121–122.

10. Ibid., 123–124.

11. Smithwick, *Evolution of a State*, 72, 75.

12. Andrew Forest Muir, ed., *Texas in 1837, an Anonymous Contemporary Narrative*, 94–99; Samuel A. Maverick, *Notes on the Storming of Bexar in the close of 1835*, 8; Jesús F. de la Teja and John Wheat, "Bexar: Profile of a Tejano Community, 1820–1832," *Southwestern Historical Quarterly* 89 (July 1985): 7–34.

13. J. H. Kuykendall as quoted in Cleburne Huston, *Deaf Smith: Incredible Texas Spy*, 94; Jenkins, *Papers of the Texas Revolution*, I, 18–19, 25–26, 36, 45, 62, 78, 87, 102, 129, 138, 248, 275–277, 283, 300, 406;

Reports of Mexican Military Units at San Antonio, Béxar Archives, Microfilm, Southwest Collection, Texas Tech University, roll 165, frame 668, roll 166, frames 79–80, 99, roll 167, frames 70, 135–147, 167.

14. Jenkins, *Papers of the Texas Revolution*, I, 408, 467, 497, II, 77–78, 110–111; Maverick, *Notes on the Storming of Bexar*, 8–9; Reports of Mexican Military Units at San Antonio, Béxar Archives, Microfilm, roll 167, frames 70, 135–147; Vicente Filisola, *The History of the War in Texas*, II, 59.

15. Stanley C. Green, *The Mexican Republic: The First Decade, 1823–1832*, 82–84, 183–186.

16. Jenkins, *Papers of the Texas Revolution*, I, 408; José Enrique de la Peña, *With Santa Anna in Texas*, 8, 21; Christian I. Archer, *The Army in Bourbon Mexico, 1760–1810*, 300–301.

17. Richard G. Santos, *Santa Anna's Campaign against Texas in 1835–1836*, 34–35; Jenkins, *Papers of the Texas Revolution*, II, 78; J. M. Rodriguez, *Memoirs*, 7; Maverick, *Notes on the Storming of Bexar*, 22; Michael Robert Green, "El Soldado Mexicano, 1835–1836," *Military History of Texas and the Southwest* 13, no. 1: 5–10.

3. ADVANCE TO CONCEPCIÓN

1. Jenkins, *Papers of the Texas Revolution*, II, 127–128, 133; Muir, *Texas in 1837*, 93; Smithwick, *Evolution of a State*, 75; Pohl and Hardin, "Military History of the Texas Revolution," 285; Jane Bradfield, *Rx Take One Cannon: The Gonzales Come and Take It Cannon of October, 1835*.

2. Jenkins, *Papers of the Texas Revolution*, II, 114–115, 138–139, 142–143, 151–154; Maverick, *Notes on the Storming of Bexar*, 9; Smithwick, *Evolution of a State*, 76.

3. Jenkins, *Papers of the Texas Revolution*, II, 151–153, 162–164; Wooten, *Comprehensive History of Texas*, I, 544; Weekly Return of Col. John H. Moore's Regiment for 21 October 1835, Austin Papers, Series IV.

4. Maverick, *Notes on the Storming of Bexar*, 8–11; Jenkins, *Papers of the Texas Revolution*, II, 111–112, 133, 145.

5. Jenkins, *Papers of the Texas Revolution*, II, 138, 172–173; Wooten, *Comprehensive History of Texas*, I, 545; Muir, *Texas in 1837*, 94; J. Frank Dobie, "Jim Bowie, Big Dealer," *Southwestern Historical Quarterly* 60 (January 1957): 337–357; Huston, *Deaf Smith*, 1–16; Lawrence D. Williams, "Deaf Smith: Scout of the Texas Revolution" (M.A. thesis, Trinity University, 1964), 3–12, 25–26.

6. Jenkins, *Papers of the Texas Revolution*, II, 50, 189, 196, 199, 208; Juan N. Seguin and others to Stephen H. Darden, January 12, 1875, with list of Béxar County soldiers in the battle of San Antonio, Casiano-Perez Papers, Daughters of the Republic of Texas Library, San Antonio, reprinted in James M. Day, ed., "Texan Letters and Documents," *Texana* 5

(Spring 1967): 81–84; John N. Seguin, *Personal Memoirs*, 7–8, reprinted in David J. Weber, ed., *Northern Mexico on the Eve of the United States Invasion;* List of Militia marching to Monclova, May 15, 1835, Béxar Archives, Microfilm, roll 165, frame 143; Webb, Carroll, Branda, eds., *Handbook of Texas*, I, 145–146, II, 589–590.

7. Ruby Cumby Smith, "James W. Fannin Jr. in the Texas Revolution," *Southwestern Historical Quarterly* 23 (October 1919): 80–84.

8. Jenkins, *Papers of the Texas Revolution*, II, 187–188, 190–191; Muir, *Texas in 1837*, 94.

9. Jenkins, *Papers of the Texas Revolution*, II, 189, 202–203, 206.

10. Ibid., II, 111, 164–165, 202–204, 207, 209; Maverick, *Notes on the Storming of Bexar*, 9–10; Creed Taylor, *Tall Men with Long Rifles*, 33–34; Béxar Archives, Microfilm, roll 167, frames 231, 236, 251–253, 259–262, 370–371.

11. Wooten, *Comprehensive History of Texas*, I, 546–547; Smithwick, *Evolution of a State*, 76; Jenkins, *Papers of the Texas Revolution*, II, 222–223; Taylor, *Tall Men with Long Rifles*, 31–32; Llerena Friend, *Sam Houston, the Great Designer*, 1–63. Henderson Yoakum in his *History of Texas*, reprinted in Wooten, *Comprehensive History of Texas*, I, 184–185, declares that Austin suggested that Houston assume direction of the army, but Houston refused because the volunteers had chosen Austin. Moses Austin Bryan, in Wooten, I, 547, says the offer was never made. Moseley Baker and Robert Coleman, critics of Houston, later accused him of unsuccessfully seeking to become the leader of the army in October 1835 and of attempting suicide when he failed. Moseley Baker to Sam Houston, October 1844, Barker Texas History Center, University of Texas at Austin; Robert M. Coleman, *Houston Displayed; or, Who Won the Battle of San Jacinto?* 5–7.

12. Jenkins, *Papers of the Texas Revolution*, II, 222–223, 248–249; Amasa Turner, "Reminiscences Concerning the Texas Revolution," Amasa Turner Papers, Barker Texas History Center, University of Texas at Austin.

13. Jenkins, *Papers of the Texas Revolution*, II, 220, 221; Wooten, *Comprehensive History of Texas*, I, 548; Filisola, *History of the War in Texas*, II, 67.

14. Jenkins, *Papers of the Texas Revolution*, II, 230, 231.

15. Moses Austin Bryan, "Recollections of Stephen F. Austin," 15, Bryan Papers; Smithwick, *Evolution of a State*, 77; Jenkins, *Papers of the Texas Revolution*, II, 243; Wooten, *Comprehensive History of Texas*, I, 549.

16. Wooten, *Comprehensive History of Texas*, I, 186, 550; Jenkins, *Papers of the Texas Revolution*, II, 254–255; Smithwick, *Evolution of a State*, 77; Sherwood Y. Reams Letter, 1836, Barker Texas History Center, University of Texas at Austin.

17. Smithwick, *Evolution of a State*, 77; Wooten, *Comprehensive His-*

tory of Texas, I, 550; Jenkins, *Papers of the Texas Revolution*, II, 254–255; Filisola, *History of the War in Texas*, II, 67.

18. Smithwick, *Evolution of a State*, 80; Wooten, *Comprehensive History of Texas*, I, 551; Joseph E. Field, *Three Years in Texas, Including a View of the Texas Revolution*, 15–16; Jenkins, *Papers of the Texas Revolution*, II, 242–245, 254–255; Filisola, *History of the War in Texas*, II, 68.

19. Wooten, *Comprehensive History of Texas*, I, 549, 552.

20. Ibid., I, 551; Jenkins, *Papers of the Texas Revolution*, II, 242–243; Smithwick, *Evolution of a State*, 77, 80.

21. Jenkins, *Papers of the Texas Revolution*, II, 242–245, 254–255; Maverick, *Notes on the Storming of Bexar*, 12; Military Copy Book, 1831–1835, José Juan Sánchez Navarro Papers, Barker Texas History Center, University of Texas at Austin; David Glenn Hunt, "Vito Alessio Robles: Coahuila y Texas, Desde la Consumación de la Independencia Hasta el Tratado de Paz de Guadalupe Hidalgo (Mexico, 1946) an Edited Translation of Volume II, Chapters 1–7" (M.A. thesis, Southern Methodist University, 1950), 64–65; Filisola, *History of the War in Texas*, II, 68.

4. ENCIRCLEMENT

1. Jenkins, *Papers of the Texas Revolution*, I, 26–27, 82–83, 183–184, II, 243, 233, 247, 251, 295, 298–299; Wooten, *Comprehensive History of Texas*, I, 554; Mary Whatley Clarke, *Thomas J. Rusk: Soldier, Statesman, Jurist*, 3–19.

2. Jenkins, *Papers of the Texas Revolution*, II, 271–273, 287–288, 290, 298–299; Wooten, *Comprehensive History of Texas*, I, 554–555.

3. Jenkins, *Papers of the Texas Revolution*, II, 294–297, 300–302, 248, 274, 305–306, 310–311; Taylor, *Tall Men with Long Rifles*, 44; Undated "Notes on Bejar," Thomas J. Rusk Papers, Barker Texas History Center, University of Texas at Austin.

4. Jenkins, *Papers of the Texas Revolution*, II, 304–306, 310–311, 318–319, 320–322; Smithwick, *Evolution of a State*, 81; Daughters of the Republic of Texas, *Muster Rolls of the Texas Revolution*, 46–47; Moses Austin Bryan, "Recollections of Stephen F. Austin," 17, Bryan Papers; Petition to the Officers of the Army of the People now before San Antonio, November 13, 1835, Rusk Papers.

5. Jenkins, *Papers of the Texas Revolution*, II, 221, 230, 341; Archie P. McDonald, *Travis*, 130–134; *Heroes of Texas*, 131.

6. Wooten, *Comprehensive History of Texas*, I, 554.

7. Jenkins, *Papers of the Texas Revolution*, II, 338–339.

8. Ibid., II, 333–334, 341, 344–345, 349–350, 355–356, 362; "Notes on Bejar," Rusk Papers; Returns of the Elections for Colonel and Lieutenant Colonel, November 5–7, 1835, Return of the Election held in the Red Land Companies for Major of the Battalion, November 7, 1835, Austin

Papers, Series IV. The colonel's election is listed in Jenkins, *Papers of the Texas Revolution*, II, 496, but is misdated November 24 which followed the editors of the *Lamar Papers*.

9. Jenkins, *Papers of the Texas Revolution*, II, 378; Maverick, *Notes on the Storming of Bexar*, 16; Robert Hunter, *Narrative of Robert Hancock Hunter, 1813–1902*, 37–38.

10. Jenkins, *Papers of the Texas Revolution*, II, 334, 364, 376–377, 381, 442.

11. Ibid., II, 405, 442–443.

12. Ibid., II, 413, 372, 381; Maverick, *Notes on the Storming of Bexar*, 14–18.

13. Jenkins, *Papers of the Texas Revolution*, II, 406, 407, 417–419, 446–447, 456–457.

14. Ibid., II, 396–397, 457–460, 486; McDonald, *Travis*, 139–142.

15. Jenkins, *Papers of the Texas Revolution*, II, 427–431.

16. Ibid., II, 399–401, 428–429.

17. Ibid., II, 407–408, 413–414, 464–465; Ralph W. Steen, "Analysis of the Work of the General Council of Texas, 1835–1836," *Southwestern Historical Quarterly* 41 (April 1938): 324–327.

18. Jenkins, *Papers of the Texas Revolution*, II, 434–435, 444–445; Maverick, *Notes on the Storming of Bexar*, 20; Herman Ehrenberg, *With Milam and Fannin*, 43–44.

19. Jenkins, *Papers of the Texas Revolution*, II, 445, 450, 452–453.

20. Ibid., II, 446, 447, 455, 479, 480, 486, 487, 489; Wooten, *Comprehensive History of Texas*, I, 556–557; Maverick, *Notes on the Storming of Bexar*, 21.

21. Wooten, *Comprehensive History of Texas*, I, 557–559. In using the account by William T. Austin, in Wooten, with regard to the actions of William H. Wharton, one should be aware that Austin had fought a duel with John A. Wharton in 1834. William Ransom Hogan, *The Texas Republic*, 275.

22. Jenkins, *Papers of the Texas Revolution*, II, 450–451, 495, 496, III, 160–161; Moses Austin Bryan, "Recollections of Stephen F. Austin," 22, Bryan Papers.

23. *A Brief History of the Burleson Family*, 31–35; Ann Hubbard Gaddis, "Edward Burleson: Frontiersman of the Texas Republic, 1798–1851" (M.A. thesis, Trinity University, 1970), 1–4; Eugene C. Barker, "The San Jacinto Campaign," *Southwestern Historical Quarterly* 4 (April 1901): 295.

24. Daughters of the Republic of Texas, *Muster Rolls of the Texas Revolution*, 43, 45–46; Ehrenberg, *With Milam and Fannin*, 1–36; Karl Wilson Baker, "Following the New Orleans Greys," *Southwest Review* 22 (1937): 213–229; M. L. Crimmins, ed., "The Storming of San Antonio de Bexar in 1835," *West Texas Historical Association Year Book* 22 (1946):

96–101; Election of Officers by the New Orleans Volunteer Greys at Quintana, October 26, 1835, M. L. Crimmins Papers, Barker Texas History Center, University of Texas at Austin.

25. Ehrenberg, *With Milam and Fannin,* 47–56; Daniel Shipman, *Frontier Life,* 74.

26. Filisola, *History of the War in Texas,* II, 58, 69–73; Charles H. Harris III, *A Mexican Family Empire: The Latifundio of the Sanchez Navarros, 1765–1867,* 136, 284.

27. Jenkins, *Papers of the Texas Revolution,* III, 5–8; Frank W. Johnson, *A History of Texas and Texans,* I, 347–349; Maverick, *Notes on the Storming of Bexar,* 22; Taylor, *Tall Men with Long Rifles,* 47–48. Burleson reported fifteen Mexican dead on the field (Jenkins, *Papers of the Texas Revolution,* III, 5–6) while Cos thought his artillery had inflicted heavy losses. Mexican cavalry companies lost two killed and eight wounded (Military Copy Book, 1831–1835, Sánchez Navarro Papers). Samuel C. A. Rogers, Reminiscences, 15, Samuel C. A. Rogers Papers, Eugene C. Barker Texas History Center, University of Texas at Austin.

5. ATTACK AND DEFENSE

1. Jenkins, *Papers of the Texas Revolution,* II, 496, III, 31–32, 43–44, 49–50, 64, 227; George B. Erath, *Memoirs of Major George B. Erath, 1813–1891,* 26; Clarke, *Rusk,* 21; Samuel C. A. Rogers, Reminiscences, 16–17.

2. Harry Warren, "Col. William G. Cooke," *Southwestern Historical Quarterly* 9 (January 1906): 212–213; Maverick, *Notes on the Storming of Bexar,* 23; *State Gazette* (Austin), September 1, 1849.

3. Warren, "Cooke," 213; Maverick, *Notes on the Storming of Bexar,* 23–24; Muster Rolls of the First and Second Divisions in the attack on San Antonio de Béxar, Archives, Texas State Library; Jenkins, *Papers of the Texas Revolution,* III, 389–390, 491, IV, 31; Harbert Davenport, "Captain Jesús Cuellar, Texas Cavalry, Otherwise 'Comanche,'" *Southwestern Historical Quarterly* 30 (July 1926): 56–62; Huston, *Deaf Smith,* 34–35; Hobart Huson, *Captain Phillip Dimmitt's Commandancy of Goliad, 1835–1836,* 175; Allen F. Adams, "The Leader of the Volunteer Greys: The Life of William G. Cooke, 1808–1847" (M.A. thesis, Southwest Texas State College, 1940), 1–6. The size of the Mexican army is based on calculations from Maverick, *Notes on the Storming of Bexar,* 9–23. The Milam quotation first appeared in the *State Gazette* (Austin), September 1, 1849, although an earlier version is given in Henry Stuart Foote, *Texas and the Texans,* II, 165.

4. Lois Garver, "Benjamin Rush Milam," *Southwestern Historical Quarterly* 38 (October 1934): 79–121, 38 (January 1935): 177–202; Smithwick, *Evolution of a State,* 74.

5. Jenkins, *Papers of the Texas Revolution*, III, 160–161; Muster Rolls of the First and Second Divisions in the attack on San Antonio de Béxar; Field, *Three Years in Texas*, 18–19; James M. Day, ed., "Texan Letters and Documents," *Texana* 5 (Spring 1967): 81–84; Taylor, *Tall Men with Long Rifles*, 56.

6. Jenkins, *Papers of the Texas Revolution*, III, 186; Baker, *Texas Scrap Book*, 37.

7. Jenkins, *Papers of the Texas Revolution*, III, 161, 186, 390; Baker, *Texas Scrap Book*, 37; Field, *Three Years in Texas*, 19; Taylor, *Tall Men with Long Rifles*, 58.

8. Jenkins, *Papers of the Texas Revolution*, III, 161, 492, VI, 57.

9. Ibid., III, 161, VI, 58; *State Gazette* (Austin), September 8, 1849; Baker, *Texas Scrap Book*, 38; Crimmins, "Storming of San Antonio," 106–108, 110.

10. Jenkins, *Papers of the Texas Revolution*, III, 161, 390, VI, 58–59; Field, *Three Years in Texas*, 20; Crimmins, "Storming of San Antonio," 108–109; Taylor, *Tall Men with Long Rifles*, 60; Ehrenberg, *With Milam and Fannin*, 81–83.

11. Jenkins, *Papers of the Texas Revolution*, III, 186; Huson, *Dimmitt's Commandancy*, 168–169; C. L. Douglas, *James Bowie: The Life of a Bravo*, 175; Ehrenberg, *With Milam and Fannin*, 81–83; Filisola, *History of the War in Texas*, II, 88–89.

12. Jenkins, *Papers of the Texas Revolution*, III, 91, 98–99, 127–128, 140–141.

13. Ibid., III, 161–162, IV, 5–7; Taylor, *Tall Men with Long Rifles*, 61; Ehrenberg, *With Milam and Fannin*, 84; Sherwood Y. Reams Letter 1836; Filisola, *History of the War in Texas*, II, 89.

14. Jenkins, *Papers of the Texas Revolution*, III, 162, 390, VI, 59; Taylor, *Tall Men with Long Rifles*, 64–65; *Texas Almanac, 1860*, 40.

15. Francis W. Johnson, *A History of Texas and Texans*, I, v–vi; Smithwick, *Evolution of a State*, 43.

16. Jenkins, *Papers of the Texas Revolution*, III, 162, VI, 59; *State Gazette* (Austin), September 15, 1849.

17. Jenkins, *Papers of the Texas Revolution*, III, 334, VI, 59; Carlos Sánchez-Navarro, *La Guerra de Tejas: Memorias de un Soldado*, 96, translated in Huson, *Dimmitt's Commandancy*, 190; Miguel A. Sánchez Lamego, *The Siege and Taking of the Alamo*, 13; Hunt, "Robles: Coahuila y Texas," 65–68.

18. Jenkins, *Papers of the Texas Revolution*, III, 162–163, VI, 59–60; Fields, *Three Years in Texas*, 21.

19. Jenkins, *Papers of the Texas Revolution*, III, 187, IV, 5–7, VI, 59; Charles A. Gulick, Jr., and Winnie Allen, eds., *The Papers of Mirabeau Buonaparte Lamar*, V, 515.

20. Jenkins, *Papers of the Texas Revolution*, III, 162–163, 186; Gulick and Allen, *Lamar Papers*, V, 514.

21. Ehrenberg, *With Milam and Fannin*, 92–95.

22. Jenkins, *Papers of the Texas Revolution*, III, 155, 163, 327, 391, VI, 60; Warren, "Cooke," 213–214; Gulick and Allen, *Lamar Papers*, IV, pt. 1, 45–46; Filisola, *History of the War in Texas*, II, 90–91.

23. Jenkins, *Papers of the Texas Revolution*, III, 391; Warren, "Cooke," 214; Crimmins, "Storming of San Antonio," 112.

24. Sánchez-Navarro, *La Guerra de Tejas*, 98–101, translated in Huson, *Dimmitt's Commandancy*, 191; Crimmins, "Storming of San Antonio, 112.

25. Sánchez-Navarro, *La Guerra de Tejas*, 101–106; Jenkins, *Papers of the Texas Revolution*, III, 146–147; Huson, *Dimmitt's Commandancy*, 184–193, 195–197; Filisola, *History of the War in Texas*, II, 92–93.

26. Jenkins, *Papers of the Texas Revolution*, III, 187; Warren, "Cooke," 214; Huson, *Dimmitt's Commandancy*, 194; Taylor, *Tall Men with Long Rifles*, 68.

27. Jenkins, *Papers of the Texas Revolution*, III, 156–158.

28. Ibid., VI, 61–63.

29. Ibid., III, 492, VI, 61; Crimmins, "Storming of San Antonio," 113.

30. Jenkins, *Papers of the Texas Revolution*, III, 161–164, 188, 199–200, 240, 335, 492, IV, 31, VI, 61; José Enrique de la Peña, *With Santa Anna in Texas: A Personal Narrative of the Revolution*, 83; Malcolm D. McLean, ed., *Papers concerning Robertson's Colony in Texas*, XII, 51–52; Ehrenberg, *With Milam and Fannin*, 98; Military Copy Book, 1831–1835, José Juan Sánchez Navarro Papers, Eugene C. Barker Texas History Center, University of Texas at Austin; Siege of Béxar, Storming and Capture of, December 5–10, 1835, M. L. Crimmins Papers, Eugene C. Barker Texas History Center, University of Texas at Austin; List of Men under the command of Lt. Col. Neill at San Antonio, Thomas William Ward Papers, Eugene C. Barker Texas History Center, University of Texas at Austin.

31. John Henry Brown, *Indian Wars and Pioneers of Texas*, 396–397; Nicholas P. Hardeman, *Wilderness Calling: The Hardeman Family in the American Westward Movement, 1750–1900*, 125.

32. Fayette Robinson, *Mexico and Her Military Chieftains*, 167; James K. Greer, *Colonel Jack Hays: Texas Frontier Leader and California Builder*, 150.

6. CONCLUSIONS

1. Miller, *Bounty and Donation Land Grants of Texas*; John J. Linn, *Reminiscences of Fifty Years in Texas*, 158–159; Harbert Davenport,

"The Men of Goliad," *Southwestern Historical Quarterly* 43 (July 1939): 1–41; Phil Rosenthal and Bill Groneman, *Roll Call at the Alamo*, 79–80, lists seventy-two of the Alamo garrison as veterans of Béxar, but the evidence for twenty-one of them seems unclear.

2. Carlos E. Castañeda, *The Mexican Side of the Texas Revolution*, 56; Santos, *Santa Anna's Campaign against Texas*, 11.

3. Helen Hunnicutt, "A Mexican View of the Texas War: Memoirs of a Veteran of the Two Battles of the Alamo," *Library Chronicle of the University of Texas* 4 (Summer 1951): 60.

4. Castañeda, *Mexican Side of the Texas Revolution*, 12–13, 351; Harris, *A Mexican Family Empire*, 193, 290.

5. Jenkins, *Papers of the Texas Revolution*, IV, 60; Jack D. Eaton, *Excavations at the Alamo Shrine*, 7, 47.

6. Louis Wiltz Kemp and Sam Houston Dixon, *The Heroes of San Jacinto*.

7. Correspondence between William G. Cooke and Thomas William Ward, December 11, 1837, June 16, 1841, Ward Papers; Webb, Carroll, and Branda, eds. *Handbook of Texas*, II, 462–463; Z. T. Fulmore, *The History and Geography of Texas as Told in County Names*.

8. Miller, *Bounty and Donation Land Grants of Texas;* Ralph A. Wooster, "Wealthy Texans, 1860," *Southwestern Historical Quarterly* 71 (October 1967): 171–180; Ed Kilman and Theon Wright, *Hugh Roy Cullen: A Story of American Opportunity*, 20–22; Richard B. Henderson, *Maury Maverick: A Political Biography*, 4; Adrian N. Anderson, "Albert Sidney Burleson: A Southern Politician in the Progressive Era" (Ph.D. diss., Texas Tech University, 1967), 1–9.

9. Francis R. Lubbock, *Six Decades in Texas*, 31; Taylor, *Tall Men with Long Rifles*, 57; *Texas Almanac, 1860*, 41.

10. Richard G. Santos, "The Siege and Storming of Bexar," in *Six Flags of Texas*, 68–69.

BIBLIOGRAPHY

MANUSCRIPTS

Daughters of the Republic of Texas Library at the Alamo, San Antonio, Texas.
    Casiano-Perez Papers.
Texas General Land Office, Archives, Austin, Texas.
    Muster Roll Book.
Texas State Library, Archives Division, Austin, Texas.
    Muster Rolls, Adjutant General's Records.
University of Texas at Austin, Eugene C. Barker Texas History Center, Archives, Austin, Texas.
    Austin, Stephen F., Papers.
    Baker, Moseley, Letter.
    Béxar Archives (Microfilm, Southwest Collection, Texas Tech University).
    Bryan, Moses Austin, Papers.
    Cooke, William G., Papers.
    Crimmins, M. L., Papers.
    Reams, Sherwood Y., Letter.
    Rogers, Samuel C. A., Papers.
    Rusk, Thomas J., Papers.
    Sánchez Navarro, José Juan, Papers.
    Turner, Amasa, Papers.
    Ward, Thomas William, Papers.

BOOKS, ARTICLES, AND THESES

Adams, Allen F. "The Leader of the Volunteer Greys: The Life of William G. Cooke, 1808–1847." M.A. thesis, Southwest Texas State Teachers College, 1940.

83

BIBLIOGRAPHY

Anderson, Adrian N. "Albert Sidney Burleson: A Southern Politician in the Progressive Era." Ph.D. diss., Texas Tech University, 1967.
Archer, Christian I. *The Army in Bourbon Mexico, 1760–1810.* Albuquerque: University of New Mexico Press, 1977.
"Austin's Order Book for the Campaign of 1835, General." *Southwestern Historical Quarterly* 11 (July 1907): 1–55.
Baker, D. W. C., comp. *A Texas Scrap Book.* Austin: Steck, 1935.
Baker, Karl Wilson. "Trailing the New Orleans Greys." *Southwest Review* 22 (1937): 213–240.
Bancroft, Hubert Howe. *History of the North Mexican States and Texas.* 2 vols. New York: Arno Press, 1970.
Barker, Eugene C. *The Life of Stephen F. Austin, Founder of Texas, 1793–1836.* Austin: Texas State Historical Association, 1949.
———. "The San Jacinto Campaign." *Southwestern Historical Quarterly* 4 (April 1901): 237–345.
———. "The Texan Revolutionary Army." *Southwestern Historical Quarterly* 9 (April 1906): 227–261.
Bennet, Miles S. "The Battle of Gonzales, the 'Lexington' of the Texas Revolution." *Southwestern Historical Quarterly* 2 (April 1899): 313–316.
Bostick, Sion R. "Reminiscences." *Southwestern Historical Quarterly* 5 (October 1901): 85–96.
Brown, John Henry. *History of Texas, 1685–1892.* 2 vols. St. Louis: L. E. Daniell, 1892.
———. *Indian Wars and Pioneers of Texas.* Austin: L. E. Daniell, 1896.
Brown, Nugent E. *The Book of Nacogdoches County.* Nacogdoches: N. E. Brown, 1927.
Bugbee, Lester G. "The Old Three Hundred." *Southwestern Historical Quarterly* 1 (October 1897): 108–117.
Burleson, Solomon S. *A Brief History of the Burleson Family.* Waco: University Printing, 1889.
Castañeda, Carlos E., trans. *The Mexican Side of the Texas Revolution.* Dallas: P. L. Turner, 1928.
Chabot, Frederick C. *With the Makers of San Antonio.* San Antonio: Artes Graficas, 1937.
Clarke, Mary Whatley. *Thomas J. Rusk: Soldier, Statesman, Jurist.* Austin: Jenkins Publishing, 1971.
Coleman, Robert M. *Houston Displayed; or, Who Won the Battle of San Jacinto?* Austin: Brick Row Book Shop, 1964.
Corner, William. *San Antonio de Béxar.* San Antonio: Bainbridge and Corner, 1890.
Crimmins, M. L., ed. "The Storming of San Antonio de Bexar in 1835." *West Texas Historical Association Year Book* 22 (1946): 95–117.

84

Curry, Ora Mae. "The Texan Siege of San Antonio, 1835." M.A. thesis, University of Texas at Austin, 1927.

Daughters of the Republic of Texas. *Muster Rolls of the Texas Revolution.* Austin: Daughters of the Republic of Texas, 1986.

Davenport, Harbert. "Captain Jesús Cuellar, Texas Cavalry, Otherwise 'Comanche.'" *Southwestern Historical Quarterly* 30 (July 1926): 56–62.

————. "The Men of Goliad." *Southwestern Historical Quarterly* 43 (July 1939): 1–41.

Day, James M., ed. "Texan Letters and Documents." *Texana* 5 (Spring 1967): 81–84.

De la Teja, Jesús F., and John Wheat. "Bexar: Profile of a Tejano Community, 1820–1832." *Southwestern Historical Quarterly* 89 (July 1985): 7–34.

Dewees, W. B. *Letters from an Early Settler of Texas.* Waco: Texian Press, 1968.

Dobie, J. Frank. "Jim Bowie, Big Dealer." *Southwestern Historical Quarterly* 60 (January 1957): 337–357.

Douglas, C. L. *James Bowie: The Life of a Bravo.* Dallas: Upshaw, 1944.

Eaton, Jack D. *Excavations at the Alamo Shrine.* San Antonio: University of Texas at San Antonio, 1980.

Ehrenberg, Herman. *With Milam and Fannin.* Dallas: Tandy Publishing, 1935.

Erath, George B. *Memoirs of Major George B. Erath, 1813–1891.* Waco: Heritage Society of Waco, 1956.

Field, Joseph E. *Three Years in Texas, Including a View of the Texas Revolution.* Austin: Steck, 1935.

Filisola, Vicente. *Memoirs for the History of the War in Texas.* Translated by Wallace Woolsey. 2 vols. Austin: Eakin Press, 1986–1987.

Foote, Henry Stuart. *Texas and the Texans.* 2 vols. Philadelphia: Thomas, Cowperthwait, 1841.

Friend, Llerena. *Sam Houston, The Great Designer.* Austin: University of Texas Press, 1954.

Fulmore, Z. T. *The History and Geography of Texas as Told in County Names.* Austin: Steck, 1915.

Gaddis, Ann Hubbard. "Edward Burleson: Frontiersman of the Texas Republic, 1798–1851." M.A. thesis, Trinity University, 1970.

Garver, Lois. "Benjamin Rush Milam." *Southwestern Historical Quarterly* 38 (October 1934): 79–121, 38 (January 1935): 177–202.

Green, Michael Robert. "El Soldado Mexicano, 1835–1836." *Military History of Texas and the Southwest* 13, no. 1: 5–10.

Green, Rena Maverick, ed. *Samuel Maverick, Texan, 1803–1870.* San Antonio: Privately printed, 1952.

Green, Stanley C. *The Mexican Republic: The First Decade, 1823–1832.* Pittsburgh: University of Pittsburgh Press, 1987.

Greer, James K. *Colonel Jack Hays: Texas Frontier Leader and California Builder.* College Station: Texas A&M University Press, 1987.

Hardeman, Nicholas P. *Wilderness Calling: The Hardeman Family in the American Westward Movement, 1750–1900.* Knoxville: University of Tennessee Press, 1977.

Harris, Charles H., III. *A Mexican Family Empire: The Latifundio of the Sánchez Navarros, 1765–1867.* Austin: University of Texas Press, 1975.

Henderson, Richard B. *Maury Maverick: A Political Biography.* Austin: University of Texas Press, 1970.

Heroes of Texas. Waco: Texian Press, 1966.

Hogan, William R. *The Texas Republic: A Social and Economic History.* Austin: University of Texas Press, 1969.

Houston, Andrew Jackson. *Texas Independence.* Houston: Anson Jones Press, 1938.

Hunnicutt, Helen. "A Mexican View of the Texas War: Memoirs of a Veteran of the Two Battles of the Alamo." *Library Chronicle of the University of Texas* 4 (Summer 1951): 59–74.

Hunt, David Glenn. "Vito Alessio Robles: Coahuila y Texas, desde la Consumación de la Independencia Hasta el Tratado de Paz de Guadalupe Hidalgo (Mexico, 1946), an Edited Translation of Volume II, Chapters 1–7." M.A. thesis, Southern Methodist University, 1950.

Hunter, Robert H. *Narrative of Robert Hancock Hunter, 1813–1902.* Austin: Cook Printing, 1936.

Huson, Hobart. *Captain Phillip Dimmitt's Commandancy of Goliad, 1835–1836.* Austin: Von Boeckmann-Jones, 1974.

Huston, Cleburne. *Deaf Smith: Incredible Texas Spy.* Waco: Texian Press, 1973.

Jenkins, John H., ed. *The Papers of the Texas Revolution, 1835–1836.* 10 vols. Austin: Presidial Press, 1973.

Johnson, Frank W. *A History of Texas and Texans.* Edited by Eugene C. Barker and Ernest W. Winkler. 5 vols. Chicago and New York: American Historical Society, 1914.

Kemp, Louis Wiltz, and Sam Houston Dixon. *The Heroes of San Jacinto.* Houston: Anson Jones Press, 1932.

Kilman, Ed, and Theon Wright. *Hugh Roy Cullen: A Story of American Opportunity.* New York: Prentice-Hall, 1954.

Lamar, Mirabeau Buonaparte. *Papers.* Edited by Charles A. Gulick, Jr., and Winnie Allen. 6 vols. Austin: Pemberton Press, 1968.

Linn, John J. *Reminiscences of Fifty Years in Texas.* New York: D. and J. Sadlier, 1883.

Lord, Walter. *A Time to Stand.* New York: Harper and Row, 1961.

Lubbock, Francis R. *Six Decades in Texas*. Austin: Ben C. Jones, 1900.

McDonald, Archie P. *Travis*. Austin: Pemberton Press, 1976.

McLean, Malcolm D., ed. *Papers concerning Robertson's Colony in Texas*. 13 vols. Arlington: University of Texas at Arlington, 1974–1987.

Maverick, Samuel A. *Notes on the Storming of Bexar in the Close of 1835*. San Antonio: Frederick C. Chabot, 1942.

Miller, Thomas Lloyd. *Bounty and Donation Land Grants of Texas, 1835–1888*. Austin: University of Texas Press, 1967.

Muir, Andrew Forest, ed. *Texas in 1837: An Anonymous, Contemporary Narrative*. Austin: University of Texas Press, 1958.

Mullins, Marion Day, ed. *The First Census of Texas, 1829–1836*. Washington: National Genealogical Society, 1959.

Owsley, Frank Lawrence, Jr. *Struggle for the Gulf Borderlands: The Creek War and the Battle of New Orleans, 1812–1815*. Gainesville: University Presses of Florida, 1981.

Peña, José Enrique de la. *With Santa Anna in Texas: A Personal Narrative of the Revolution*. College Station: Texas A&M University Press, 1975.

Pohl, James W., and Stephen L. Hardin. "The Military History of the Texas Revolution: An Overview." *Southwestern Historical Quarterly* 89 (January 1986): 269–308.

Robinson, Fayette. *Mexico and Her Military Chieftains*. Glorieta, N.M.: Rio Grande Press, 1970.

Rodriguez, J. M. *Memoirs*. San Antonio: Standard Printing, 1961.

Sánchez Lamego, Miguel A. *The Siege and Taking of the Alamo*. Translated by Consuelo Velasco. Santa Fe: Press of the Territorian, 1968.

Sánchez-Navarro, Carlos. *La Guerra de Tejas: Memorias de un Soldado*. Mexico City: Editorial Polis, 1938.

Santos, Richard G. *Santa Anna's Campaign against Texas in 1835–1836*. Waco: Texian Press, 1968.

———. "The Siege and Storming of Bexar." In *Six Flags of Texas*. Waco: Texian Press, 1968.

Seguin, Juan N. *Personal Memoirs*. Reprinted in David J. Weber, ed., *Northern Mexico on the Eve of the United States Invasion*. New York: Arno Press, 1976.

Shipman, Daniel. *Frontier Life*. Houston: N.p., 1879; reprinted Pasadena, Tex.: Abbotsford Publishing, 1965.

Smith, Ruby Cumby. "James W. Fannin, Jr., in the Texas Revolution." *Southwestern Historical Quarterly* 23 (October 1919): 80–90, 23 (January, 1920): 171–205, 23 (April, 1920): 271–284.

Smithwick, Noah. *The Evolution of a State; or, Recollections of Old Texas Days*. Austin: University of Texas Press, 1983.

State Gazette. Austin. September 1, 8, 15, 1849.

Steen, Ralph W. "Analysis of the Work of the General Council of Texas,

1835–1836." *Southwestern Historical Quarterly* 41 (April 1938): 324–348.

Taylor, Creed. *Tall Men with Long Rifles.* San Antonio: Naylor, 1935.

Teja, Jesús F. de la. *See* De la Teja, Jesús F.

Terrell, Alex. W. "Stephen F. Austin: A Memorial Address." *Southwestern Historical Quarterly* 14 (January 1911): 182–197.

Texas Almanac, 1860. Galveston, Richardson, 1860.

Thrall, Homer S. *Pictorial History of Texas.* St. Louis: Woodward and Tiernan, 1878.

Urwitz, Marie Bennet. "Valentine Bennet." *Southwestern Historical Quarterly* 9 (January 1906): 145–156.

Warren, Harry. "Col. William G. Cooke." *Southwestern Historical Quarterly* 9 (January 1906): 210–219.

Webb, Walter P., H. Bailey Carroll, and Eldon Branda, eds. *The Handbook of Texas.* 3 vols. Austin: Texas State Historical Association, 1952–1976.

Weber, David J. *The Mexican Frontier, 1821–1846: The American Southwest under Mexico.* Albuquerque: University of New Mexico Press, 1982.

White, Gifford. *Character Certificates in the General Land Office of Texas.* St. Louis: Inquire Publications, 1985.

———. *The 1840 Census of the Republic of Texas.* Austin: Pemberton Press, 1966.

———. *1830 Citizens of Texas.* Austin: Eakin Press, 1983.

Williams, Lawrence D. "Deaf Smith: Scout of the Texas Revolution." M.A. thesis, Trinity University, 1964.

Williams, Villamae, ed. *Stephen F. Austin's Register of Families.* Nacogdoches: Ericson Books, 1984.

Wooten, Dudley G. *A Comprehensive History of Texas, 1685 to 1897.* 2 vols. Austin: Texas State Historical Association, 1986.

Yoakum, Henderson. *History of Texas.* 2 vols. Austin: Steck, 1935.

INDEX

Borden, Thomas W.: company of, 49, 68, 71
Bowie, James, ix, 31; background of, 17; as commander, 18–19, 22–26, 28–29, 39, 60–61, 70; left army, 41
Bradley, John M.: company of, 49, 68, 71
Brazoria, 37–38; company from, 53
Brazos River, 38, 63
Breece, Thomas H., 38; company of, 45, 71
Briscoe, Andrew, 9; company of, 22, 32, 70
British weapons, 14
Bryan, Moses Austin, 6, 37
Burleson, Edward, 7, 21, 31–32, 34; background of, 37; as commander, 36–44, 49, 53–54, 56, 58, 61–62, 65, 67, 69–71; family of, 65
Burleson, James, 40
Burnet, David, 44

Caldwell, Matthew, 8; company of, 70
Cameron, John, 56
Camp Defiance, 32
Canada, 37
cannon. See artillery
Catholic church, 1
cavalry, ix; Mexican, viii, 4, 8, 12–16, 18, 21, 24–25, 39–40, 52–53, 55, 57, 64, 68, 69, 72; Texan, 25, 29–33, 39–40, 49
Central Texas, 15
Cheshire, James: company of, 49, 53, 67–68, 71
Cibolo Creek, 15, 16, 17, 29
civilians, 16, 33, 57, 64
Coahuila, 12, 44
Coleman, Robert M., 8, 9, 41,

76; company of, 22, 24, 49, 68, 70, 71
Colorado River, 8, 63
Columbia, 9
comet, 17
Concepción mission, vii, 22; battle of, viii, 23–26, 60–61, 63, 69
Condelle, Nicolás, 13, 33, 54–56, 63
Confederation period, 2
Constitution of 1824, 18, 56, 64
Consultation, 18, 20, 21, 29
Convention of 1832, 2, 51
Convention of 1833, 2, 37
Cooke, William, 44, 54, 56, 62, 65, 69; company of, 45, 53, 71
Copano Bay, 12
cornfield, 46
Cos, Martín Perfecto de, viii, ix, 9; background of, 12; as commander, 12–13, 16–23, 26–28, 32–33, 36, 39–42, 46, 49–50, 52–58, 62–65, 68–70
Cos house, viii
counties: named for veterans of San Antonio, 65
Crane, John: company of, 45, 50, 51, 71
Creek war, 9
Cuellar, Jesús "Comanche," 42
Cullen, Ezekiel W.: family of, 65
cultural conflict, 4
customs duties, 2, 9, 12, 30

Dance, Henry, 57
de la Garza, Father Refugio, 53–54, 56
de la Garza home, 46, 50
DeWitt, Green: colony of, volunteers from, 8
Duncan, Peter J.: company of, 45, 53, 71

Lipantitlán, 13
Llewellyn, Thomas: company of, 45, 51, 71
Lockhart, Byrd: company of, 32, 70
Logan, Greenberry, 57
Long, James, 44
Louisiana, 8, 37, 44
Lubbock, Thomas, 66

McDonald, William, 50
Main Plaza, 11, 46
Martin, Albert, 8
Matamoros, 30, 41, 62
Maverick, Samuel, 33, 41, 44, 45, 68–69; family of, 65
Medina River, 32, 34
Mendosa, José María, 24
Mexía, José Antonio, 30
Mexican army, viii; casualties, 19, 26, 40, 50, 57–58, 69; morale, ix, 14, 18, 27, 35, 49, 55, 58–59, 64; officers, 12–14, 63; order of battle, 72; reinforcements, 33, 39, 51–52, 54–55; size, ix, 12–13, 20, 42–44, 49, 68–70; supplies, 12, 39, 58–59, 63; surrender, 56–58; weapons, 14, 56, 58. See also artillery; cavalry; Morelos Battalion
Mexican Texans, 11–12, 18, 19, 30, 31, 35, 48, 64, 65
Mexico: government of, 1–5; independence celebration in, 11–12; revolution in, 14
Mier, Mexico: battle of, 58
Milam, Ben, 15; background of, 44; as commander, 44–46, 49, 58, 62, 71; killed, 50
Military Plaza, 11
militia, 29
mill. See sugarcane mill
Mississippi: company from, 38

Missouri, 37, 51
Monterrey, Mexico: battle of, 58
Moore, John H., 7, 8, 28, 29, 31, 70
Morelos Battalion, 12–14, 24–26, 39–40, 49–58, 63, 68–72
Morris, Robert C., 38, 42, 45, 51, 56
mules, 19

Nacogdoches, 2, 20, 38; battle of, 10, 17; company from, 10, 27
Natchitoches, Louisiana, 38
Navarro, Antonio: home of, 51, 52
Navarro ranch, 42
Neill, James C., 67–68; company of, 16, 45, 70, 71
New Orleans Greys, 37–38, 44, 45, 53
North, 8, 37
North Carolina, 37
Nueces River, 13, 33
Nuevo León: company from, 13, 72

Old Stone Fort, 10
Old Three Hundred settlers, 8

Parrott, T. L. F.: company of, 67, 70
Patton, William: company of, 45, 53, 71
Peacock, J. W.: company of, 45, 71
physicians, 58
presidial cavalry. See cavalry, Mexican
priest, 26, 28
Protestant religion, 1
Pueblo: company from, 72

racial conflict, 4, 18
"Redlanders," 27
religion, 1

Rio Grande, 30, 32
Río Grande: company from,
13, 72
Roberts, John S.: company of, 45,
49, 68, 71
Robinson, James, 34
Rusk, Thomas J., ix, 31, 34, 39–
40, 65; background of, 27; left
army, 41; company of, 70
Ruth, Michael: company of, 49,
68, 71

Salado Creek, 16, 17, 19, 61
Salinas Ranch, 32
Saltillo, 15, 39, 51
San Antonio, vii–ix; access to,
controlled, 17; appearance and
population of, 11, 57; battle for,
41–59, 60–66; fortifications at,
16–17, 25; military importance
of, 4, 13, 64; siege of, 27–40
San Antonio de Valero mission.
See Alamo
San Antonio River, vii, 11, 19, 33,
41, 45–46, 48–50, 53, 57
San Augustine, 38, 51
Sánchez Lamego, Miguel G., 69
Sánchez Navarro, José Juan, 39,
51–52, 54–56, 63, 64, 69
San Felipe, 18, 20, 30, 51, 58;
Committee of Safety at, 7, 10;
company from, 9
San Fernando church, 11, 13, 48
San Jacinto: battle cry, vii; battle-
field, viii; battle of, 61, 64, 65;
veterans of San Antonio at, 65
San José mission, 19, 22
San Juan mission, 19, 22
San Miguel Creek, 32
San Pedro Creek, 11, 50
Santa Anna, Antonio López de,
viii, 2–4, 6, 12, 19; strategy of,
ix, 64
Santos, Richard, 66

Seguín, Erasmo, 18
Seguín, Juan N., 18, 30, 62; com-
pany of, 49, 68, 70, 71
Shipman, Daniel, 38
sickness, 29
slavery, 4
slave smuggling, 18
Smith, Benjamin, 28
Smith, Erastus ("Deaf"), 38, 39,
45, 46; background of, 17;
wounded, 48
Smith, Henry, 49
Smith, John W., 33, 41, 42, 44,
45, 53
Smithwick, Noah, 7, 22, 25
Somervell, Alexander, 7, 31,
32, 42
South, 8, 37
South Carolina, 27, 30
South Texas, 15
Splann, Peyton: company of, 49,
68, 71
Sublett, Philip A., 31, 36
sugarcane mill, 29, 45, 49
supplies. *See* Mexican army;
Texan army
Sutherland, William: company of,
53, 67, 71
Swisher, James G., 8, 39–40, 56;
company of, 45, 53, 70, 71

Tamaulipas, 12; companies from,
13, 55, 72
Tampico, 30
taxes, 2
Taylor, Creed, 45, 69
Tennessee, 8, 37, 55
Texan army, viii; advance on San
Antonio, vii, viii, 15–26; casualties, 26, 40, 49–52, 57; celebrate victory, 57; discipline, 29,
33, 41, 62; first division, 45–
46, 71; morale, 29, 30–31, 33,
35, 41–42, 50; officers, 7, 28,